PYRE

PRAISE FOR PERUMAL MURUGAN

TWICE LONGLISTED FOR THE NATIONAL BOOK AWARD FOR TRANSLATED LITERATURE

'It's not just the physical world Murugan describes so vividly . . . but the rural community, a village of 20 huts and a thousand ancient resentments . . . I'm hoping for a whole shelf of books from this writer' Parul Sehgal, *New York Times* on *One Part Woman*

'Sometimes shocking, but in a way that always encourages understanding . . . Murugan writes with both empathy and compassion' *Times Literary Supplement* on *One Part Woman*

'*The Story of a Goat* . . . jumps nimbly from fantasy to realism to parable . . . The effect is not so much escapist fantasy as existential reflection . . . The elegance of Murugan's simple tone will lull you deeper into his story' Ron Charles, *Washington Post*

'[A] superbly fabulist tale . . . Murugan explores the lively inner life of an observant goat in this imaginative exploration of rural life under the caste system' *Publishers Weekly* on *The Story of a Goat*

'An affecting story told with sensitivity towards the plight of the individual and calm fury at society's brutality' *Irish Times* on *The Story of a Goat*

'[Murugan] is the most accomplished of his generation of Tamil writers' *Caravan*

PYRE

PERUMAL MURUGAN

TRANSLATED FROM THE TAMIL BY
ANIRUDDHAN VASUDEVAN

pushkin press

71–75 Shelton Street
London WC2H 9JQ

Pyre was first published as *Pookkuzhi* by Kalachuvadu
Publications Pvt. Ltd, Nagercoil in 2013
First published in English by Hamish Hamilton, Penguin Books India in 2016
Published by Penguin Books, Penguin Random House India in 2017
Revised edition published by Grove Atlantic in 2022

First published by Pushkin Press in 2022

1 3 5 7 9 8 6 4 2

ISBN 13: 978-1-78227-862-7

Printed and bound by Clays Ltd, Elcograf S.p.A.

www.pushkinpress.com

CONTENTS

ONE

The sun was blazing overhead when Saroja and Kumaresan stepped off the bus.

Beyond the tamarind trees that lined the road, all they could see were vast expanses of arid land. There were no houses anywhere in sight. With each searing gust of wind, the white summer heat spread over everything as if white saris had been flung across the sky. There was not a soul on the road. Even the birds were silent. Just an ashen dryness, singed by the heat, hung in the air. Saroja hesitated to venture into that inhospitable space.

'Step down with your right foot first,' Kumaresan had said to her. She was now unsure whether he had said this in jest or if he had meant it. By habit, anyway, she had descended from the bus with her right foot first, but she was not sure he had noticed that. The courage she had gathered until then suddenly vanished, leaving her feeling uneasy. When her feet touched the ground, she had prayed within her heart, 'May everything go well.' She could not think of a specific god. She only knew the name of Kumaresan's family deity, Goddess Kali, but she would not have been able to confidently recognize the goddess's idol in the temple.

The only Kali she knew was a goddess with widened eyes, terrifying teeth and her tongue sticking out. She could not pray to that Kali, who only inspired fear.

Kumaresan had already walked quite some distance. Saroja quickly found her bearings and trotted ahead to join him. Shifting the heavy bag to his other hand, he looked at her. Nothing here appeared new to him. He was used to navigating this place even in the dark. He always walked with a spring in his step when he was here, and he felt the same way now. But *she* was new. She seemed like a lush crop of corn—perhaps a little withered and dull right now, but easily refreshed with just a drop of rain. He noticed her struggling to keep pace with him, so he slowed down, conscious of how briskly he'd been marching ahead. The very sight of her took away his anxiety and brought him some calm. He could sense that, as a girl from a crowded city, Saroja was probably terrified by the emptiness of this place.

He looked at her face. A lock of hair had escaped her plait and swayed against her cheek. He longed to gently tuck it behind her ear. He tried to control himself, but his heart's desirous reach could not be checked. His gaze still on her, he smiled and said, 'At midday, not even a crow or a sparrow ventures out in this heat. This is not a big city like yours, just a little village. But wait and see. You will be amazed at how many different people live here. Don't worry about a thing. I am here.'

Kumaresan had rehearsed his strategy several times in his head. He believed that everything would go according to plan; it had to. He had thought long and hard about all possible contingencies and modified the plan accordingly. And though he was well aware that any scheme can unravel no matter how foolproof it might have seemed at first, a blind courage propelled him on.

Saroja clutched his shoulder and continued to shuffle ahead, making sure her legs didn't get in the way of his. Smiling faintly, she wondered if he would have taken her smile to mean, 'I have no one besides you. I have come placing all my trust in you.' Perhaps he did. He somehow already understood all her movements, like someone who had known her intimately for a long time. Her grip on his shoulder slowed him down and held him back, but he savoured the pleasure of her warm grasp, and kept walking.

They were on the main road that led from Senkundroor to Odaiyur. To get to Kattuppatti, they would have to walk another mile. He kept explaining the different routes and places to her. The chatter helped him keep his anxiety in check. Though she was aware that he was describing the village's layout and other things, her attention began to drift. She had exhausted herself thinking about what might have transpired in her town, and now her mind was muddled with questions about what could happen here. All night, her imagination had terrorized her with the thought that policemen would intercept them any minute and take her away from Kumaresan. Even now, she was seized by that fear, and she kept looking about warily.

When nothing untoward happened during their journey, she wondered if her family had said good riddance to her and disowned her. Perhaps they were relieved and happy that she had not taken anything with her, that she had walked out in just the sari she was wearing. Was that all there was to it? Was that all there was to everything? Had all these years of love and affection meant nothing? Why hadn't they come looking for her? Despite her fears of being separated from Kumaresan, she would have been somewhat comforted if someone had come after them, even if it was the police. Now all she had was the emptiness of knowing no one was looking for her. After all this, could she ever go back there? And would anyone embrace her and welcome her back if she did? They would just say, 'You left. Couldn't you just stay away?'

But if she did choose to go back home after all of this, she would feel less fearful if she went with Kumaresan. In any case, he wouldn't let her go alone. He had already said enough to dispel her fear and boost her confidence. She held on to those heartfelt words he had uttered: 'If you can trust that from now on I am everything for you, then come with me.' Even if she came to lose everything else, as long as she had him it was enough. 'I am everything for you,' he had said to her. When she repeated it to him several times like a chant, he had laughed. It was a laugh of approval.

He had already explained to her that once they reached the village, he would do most of the talking, and that no matter what his mother or the others in the village asked her, she need speak only a word or two in response. He had repeated this to her several times—both when they left

Tholur together on the bus, with her head resting on his shoulder, and when they resumed their journey after they got married—to make sure she understood clearly.

'Whatever I say, amma will listen to me,' he reassured her many times in many different ways. 'She will worry about what others might say, but everything will be all right soon. Don't be afraid.'

Saroja nodded like an obedient child, hanging on to Kumaresan's every word. Although it was uncharacteristic of her garrulous nature not to talk, she realized how important it was to act according to his wishes while in the village. Later, when things had settled and she learns how things worked here, she could probably chatter as much as she wanted to. But until then she had best follow his instructions.

He even told her that he had hinted at these possibilities to his mother already. Apparently, the last time he was in the village, she had said to him, 'What do you say? Shall we start looking for a girl for you?'

'No rush,' he had replied. 'We can talk about this at leisure some other time.'

'You live in a different town. Please don't come back here dragging along a girl from a different caste,' she had said, fixing her gaze on him.

Laughing, he had responded, 'So what? If I don't find a girl for myself, you think you will? I am the one who has to live with her.'

His mother had not said anything more on the subject. He believed he had given her enough to think about. When he took his leave, she had merely grunted a non-committal 'Hmm.' He had had such conversations with her a few times already. Now he assured Saroja that his mother wouldn't be entirely shocked.

'Can anyone who looks at your face not like you, my dear?' he asked her. 'They will instantly be won over to your side. They might even forget me. "Look at this foul-mouthed fellow's luck!" the boys will say.'

Every time he called her 'my dear', she quivered in delight. Even though she couldn't tell if he actually meant it or was saying it in jest, it still made her secretly happy in her heart. The expression in his eyes was always very earnest, without any hint of exaggeration in them. If she said, 'You are fooling me,' he would surprise her with his response: 'Are you the kind of girl that gets fooled?' His very words embraced her and carried her along.

Kumaresan turned on to the mud path that forked away from the road. 'This is the royal highway that leads to our village,' he said and looked at her.

'What do you mean?' she asked. He sometimes scared her with such grandiose language. Sometimes she simply could not understand what he said. When he spoke very fast, it sounded like a whole new language to her and she would wonder if he was just being mischievous.

'A royal highway,' he explained, 'is when they lay out soft flowers for a king and his queen to walk on. Now you and I are the king and queen.' He laughed. In the heat of the day, it looked to her like the path ahead of her was strewn with long, slithering white snakes whose heads or tails she could not discern. Was this really a royal path? She felt a rush of affection for him and for the way he could joke and laugh even at such a time of anxiety.

The dust on the path stuck to their feet, searing their soles. She pulled the loose end of her sari over her head.

'Don't cover your head like that; remove it,' he said. 'In these parts, covering the head is a mark of mourning. Here, use this.' He spread a small towel over her head. Once they decided to get married, he had started saying things like 'Don't do it that way. It will be misunderstood there,' and 'This is how they do it there.' It continued even now, but she still did not know what to do and how exactly it would be perceived. She was fearful about how the villagers would interpret her actions. Every time she wondered if she would have to transform herself completely, the heaviness in her gut grew. If she had to learn everything afresh, she might as well become a child again. But who would raise her then? Was Kumaresan ready for such a prospect? She kept touching her head to make sure the towel didn't slip off.

After a while Kumaresan decided to stop under a large neem tree by the wayside. Its branches had spread over the entire width of the path, all the way to the other side, making the tree look like a giant umbrella. She looked up at it, but was unable to tell how tall the tree was; she had never seen a neem tree this huge. As soon as they halted beneath it, all her pent-up anxieties seemed to vanish, as though the tree had sucked the summer heat into itself. It was pleasant there in the shade. Glancing around the canopy, she remarked, 'What a massive tree!' She felt comforted by it, as though it had gathered her and seated her in its lap. She trusted that Kumaresan would similarly offer her refuge in his lap.

Right then, in a teasing tone, he said, 'This is my village's—no, no—*our* village's kaanakkaadu,' and pointed behind her. Confused, she looked at him. He explained, 'This is the cremation ground.'

The lap that had given her refuge only a moment ago now pushed her away and shrank back into itself. Fearfully, she looked at the cremation ground. It lay beyond the neem tree, a vast outgrowth of bushes and huge trees that rose to the sky. There was no sign of anyone being buried or cremated there. The place hid all sorts of secrets within itself, even though it appeared unassuming. Saroja turned away, but something from behind her kept its gaze on her. She wanted to leave the place.

She was familiar with the cremation ground that was part of the Tholur Municipality. It spread over acres, dotted with pits and graves. Thickets of thorny bushes had taken over some spots. There were just one or two trees, and someone or other was always lying down next to the gravestones under those trees. The racket of the men who sat huddled in the middle of the clearings amidst thorny bushes, playing cards, was a permanent feature. The place was never deserted. Her father had told her that many even slept there at night. 'They don't even let the ghosts roam around in peace,' he'd said. There was always a new pit dug out and ready in one place, and a corpse burning in another. But there was nothing of that sort here. As though he knew what she was thinking, Kumaresan said, 'Only one or two corpses are brought here every year. Most of the time, you'll only see cows and goats grazing here.'

She was trying hard to resist looking at the bushes with their closely guarded secrets when she heard a voice: 'What is it, mapillai? Why are you standing here?'

She whipped around to see a man on a bicycle, standing with one foot on the ground. He had called out to Kumaresan with a friendly term of address commonly used between men. The man was wearing a loincloth and had a towel tied around his head. He looked middle-aged, with a swollen belly and thick hair covering his entire body. Had he not been wearing the loincloth and the towel, he would have looked exactly like a dark pig. Saroja felt both embarrassed and amused at the sight of the man, but she noticed that he was sizing her up carefully. As his bee-like eyes bore into her, she lowered her gaze to protect herself from his unsettling scrutiny.

Kumaresan replied calmly, 'This is my wife, uncle. We got married just this morning.'

'Look at that! You went away to work, but you managed to find yourself a nice cow! Does your mother know?' he said, and scrutinized Saroja again from head to foot.

Saroja wondered if he would come closer and inspect her teeth. Although she was not wearing silk, she looked very much like a new bride in her new sari and blouse and with the yellow thread of the taali around her neck. Her face, strained by the exhaustion of the journey, looked like a painting shrouded in smoke. She tried to shrink her frame and hide behind Kumaresan, but the man's gaze hounded her wherever she moved.

'Amma will know only once we get home,' Kumaresan said.

'You have done something unexpected, bringing a girl from elsewhere. What caste?' the man said.

'Our caste only,' Kumaresan replied.

Since he wanted the man to leave, he kept his answers short. But it didn't look like the man had any intention of leaving. He got off his bicycle and leaned around Kumaresan to get a good look at Saroja. Seeing her struggle to hide herself, he frowned, hummed, and furrowed his eyebrows in suspicion.

'Can't I tell by the face?' he prodded relentlessly. 'This is not a face from our caste, mapillai. Does a face that wanders over fields and rocks look like this? This is the face of someone who hasn't toiled, a body that hasn't suffered summer's heat. All right, tell me the truth—whatever it is . . . Is she from our caste?'

'Yes, maama,' Kumaresan replied patiently.

Once the man realized he wouldn't be able to drag out any more information from Kumaresan, he intoned, 'All right, all right, this heat is punishing. Go home. There must be some leftover rice gruel for you to drink. Your mother might even become overjoyed at the sight of her new daughter-in-law and decide to kill a chicken and make some kozhambu and some sambar rice with cumin and everything. This is the first time such a daughter-in-law has come to our village, isn't it? Such a rare piece of sweet jaggery!' Saying this, he pedalled away, his bicycle moving slowly as its tyres pressed into the mud on the path. Saroja and Kumaresan could see the loose end of the man's loincloth dangle in the air when he hoisted himself up from the seat and pedalled with force to move faster. He turned back many times to look at them. Saroja watched with fear as the man pierced through the day's heat, leaving a trail of dust suspended in the air.

'He is from our village,' Kumaresan explained. 'We call him Podhaaru, because that is exactly what he looks like—a bush. Did you see the hair all over his body? Everyone has such a nickname. I do too, as you will find out for yourself. Anyway, now the news of our marriage will reach the village before we do. That is good in a way. We won't have to say anything. It is going be a grand welcome, you wait and see. Don't be scared by it all,' he said as he lifted the bag and placed it on his head.

'You look just like a porter,' Saroja said, looking for a distraction and trying to shake away the memory of Podhaaru's hook-like gaze. He had called her a cow, and he had stared at her just as though he was examining the animal at the country fair. Now, thinking of Kumaresan as a porter made her smile.

There were porters at Tholur railway station who scurried about carrying people's luggage. She had never travelled by train, but she was familiar with the station. Whenever she happened to pass by, she would spend a lot of time there, just standing and observing. It was one of her favourite pastimes. Their initial plan had been to leave from Tholur by train. But since they would have had to leave at a moment's notice, depending on whenever they found a good time to get away, they had abandoned that plan and decided to take the bus instead. The thought of going away by train had excited her. 'A new experience starting with a new experience,' she had thought. So she was definitely disappointed when that did not happen. He had comforted her, saying, 'It is not like we will never come back to my father-in-law's house again. We certainly will. And I will bring you by train then. Don't worry.' Concealing her tears, she had leaned on him for comfort. And when he ran his fingers gently over her cheek, she had held his hand and kept it from moving away.

'You think I look like a porter?' he said. 'Let a month or two roll by. You too will walk like this carrying a basket of dung on your head.'

Looking at the faint smile on his lips, she said, 'If you lift that weight and place it on my head, I will carry it for sure.' Her words made him happy. 'Just your saying so is enough. We will survive somehow even if we have just two cows.'

All along the way, she saw nothing but a barren landscape scorched into whiteness by the heat. Somewhere in the distance, she spotted a homestead. Thatched roofs. The two or three human figures that were out and about looked diminished from a distance. She walked with her eyes fixed on these distant figures. The path seemed endless; anyone coming here for the first time would have a difficult time finding the place. That gave her some relief.

From that endless path, they turned and started walking on a faint trail in the ground. Pointing to a group of thatched huts that sat on a large rock which looked like it had absorbed all the heat of the day, Kumaresan said, 'That is our house.' He had never said anything about his house before. She hadn't asked him either. But when she looked at the thatched hut, something in her heart came undone. To console herself, she averted her gaze and looked at the rock instead. There were no other houses in the vicinity; only some trees. She was going to find it difficult to reconcile herself to this environment.

Seeing her crestfallen expression, he said, 'Did you think it would be a house with a brick-tiled roof?'

Without lifting her face, she said, 'No, I didn't.'

'Don't worry, we can build one,' he said. This was how he was. He would never say something could not be done. Whatever it was, he'd say, 'We can do it.' It was, of course, a different matter whether he actually did it or not. But sometimes, just those words seemed enough, didn't they?

As they neared the rock, she could see the faces of the women sitting there. Their voices rose in a cacophony. As soon as they saw the couple, they all got up. Everyone was silent for a minute. Saroja stood with her head bowed, while Kumaresan set the bag on the ground and looked at them. No one said anything. There were five or six men in the crowd too.

Suddenly, from within one of the huts, there came a wail, and an aggrieved voice lashed out at them: 'You have ruined me!'

Saroja looked up to see a slender figure in a white sari standing before them, her hair undone and her hands raised in the air. Kumaresan's mother, Marayi. Saroja did not have the strength to look at her.

Marayi hit Kumaresan on his chest in protest. 'Is this why I sent you to work in a different place?' she demanded. 'I had thought my son would earn some money and walk with his head held high among the people here. But he has thrown fire on me. If he had been killed in a road accident somewhere, I would have written it off as my destiny . . . I would have cried my heart out and been done with it. But now he has given me a reason to weep for the rest of my life! Why did you do this? Why did you do this?' She clutched his shirt in her fist and slapped him repeatedly, sometimes striking his cheek and sometimes his chest. And then, turning to Saroja, she screamed, 'What did you do to bewitch my son? How many men have you done this to?'

Like someone possessed, she grabbed Saroja by her hair. Kumaresan rushed and pulled his mother away, saying, 'Let her be, Amma. What is this?'

Holding Saroja by the hand, he led her into one of the huts. They could still hear his mother wailing: 'Look at him pushing me away already! What dark magic has she cast on him! Everything is ruined. The end of my days has come about.'

The sight of the old woman sitting on the rock, wailing and beating her chest repeatedly, terrified Saroja. She wasn't even aware that she had been crying. Her body trembled with fear. Her eyes rolled up into their sockets, and the world around her faded.

'Water, water,' she mumbled.

'It is nothing, don't worry,' he kept reassuring her, but she fainted and collapsed.

TWO

Saroja's collapse panicked Kumaresan, who had caught her in his arms to break her fall.

'Amma, please bring some water!' he shouted.

There was no response from the people outside. Everyone kept looking at his mother in silence. Suddenly, she became quiet and, sitting under the neem tree by the side of the rock, began snivelling into the loose end of her sari that she held against her mouth, her body shuddering with the impact of her grief. It did not look like she had heard Kumaresan's call for help. Or if she had, she did not show it.

'Rasamma Akka, why don't you help?' Kumaresan begged the woman who was in his line of vision. 'Can you fetch some water please? She has fainted!'

But Rasamma quickly turned her face away and hid it behind the woman sitting next to her. All the others too, fearing he might call out to them for help, did the same. In the blinding heat, all he could see was a cluster of averted faces. He was filled with rage, and felt like dragging those women by their hair and throttling them. But he controlled himself. The other onlookers, whom he couldn't see from where he stood, felt safe from his angry gaze.

Kumaresan gently placed Saroja's limp body on the ground. Then he stepped outside the hut. Sweat covered his darkened face. He did not want to look at anyone. He rushed to the shack that served as the kitchen, filled some water in a jar, and ran back. He sprinkled some on her face to revive her, and then made her drink some. Seeing the terror in her darting glances, he tapped her gently on her cheek and said, 'It is nothing. Don't be afraid.'

She leaned against his chest, and whimpered.

'This is all because we walked for so long in this bare heat,' he said to her. 'I will give you some leftovers soaked in water. Would you drink that?' But she was too unsettled to respond. Leaving her alone, he went again to the kitchen and poured some of the gruel into a bowl. Stirring a few crystals of rock salt into the gruel, he went back to the hut where she was resting. 'Drink this,' he said, and placed the bowl close to her lips. After just a mouthful, she made a face and moaned, 'That's enough.'

'Drink a little more. It cools the body down,' he said.

But she did not like the smell of that gruel. Turning her face away, she said, 'No. I don't want to.'

'Drink it. It will help you,' he said, forcing her angrily.

She shook her head in refusal.

'Look here!' he raised his voice. 'Are you going to drink this or not?'

Pleadingly, she said, 'It stinks. I don't like it. It will make me vomit.'

Saroja could see that he was upset because she didn't seem to understand the value and taste of the gruel, but

she could not even take it to her lips. The smell made her
stomach churn. Belatedly, Kumaresan realized that she
might have drunk it if it had been made with rice. So he
did not force her any more, and instead drank it himself.
In Tholur, where she was from, they never mixed ragi pap
with water from grain meal soaked overnight. They only
ate pap with kozhambu. They did make porridge, but not
the kind Kumaresan was used to. They called broken rice
'noy'. And they made a porridge by cooking noy with
some flour. Here, in Kumaresan's village, however, koozh
porridge was made by boiling flour in water with some
salt. Those who were indisposed drank it lukewarm. The
porridge was supposed to fortify the body. It was even given
to cows after they delivered their calves. Having concluded
that Saroja had never tasted this gruel, he wondered what
else he could offer her to eat. It did not seem like they
had any cooked rice lying around. Even if they had rice at
home, his mother was not in the habit of cooking it often.
Finding rice was like finding gold. Once in two or three
months when she cooked meat, she would carefully measure in some rice. Or perhaps during festivals like Deepavali
or Pongal. But Saroja was used to eating rice every day.

He began to worry about how he would deal with
the food situation hereon. So far, all his plans had been
focused on managing his mother's reactions. He had not
given much thought to what else he would have to do
once Saroja began living with them. How was he going
to handle this? He was beginning to feel overwhelmed.
He looked at her lying there like a dried leaf. Usually, her

movements stirred and invited him; he always marvelled at how she managed to draw him in by merely knitting her eyebrows. But now she invoked nothing but pity in him. He could not think clearly. How am I going to take care of her here? What if she splutters and withers like a little sesame seed on this overheated rock?

Pavalayi, one of the women in the crowd outside, who had been watching his ministrations, said, 'She must be lucky to have found a husband like him, who runs about trying to take care of her.'

Another voice rose in the crowd, 'Hey, Pavala, once you go home, make sure you faint and make a scene. Your husband too might come running to take care of you!' Everyone laughed.

'Of course!' Pavalayi responded. 'Though I don't think I am good at being so dramatic. Even if I do manage to faint, he won't make me lean on his chest. Instead, he'll give me a tight slap.'

Someone else chimed in, 'Looks like we don't have to walk four or five miles and pay money to watch a film from now on. All we have to do is come and sit on this rock.'

The crowd, which now rang with the women's laughter, had grown in size. People who lived in distant fields had heard the news and were trickling in to join the throng. The new arrivals peered into the hut to take a look at Saroja, but they could not see her face clearly in the shadows. Content that she would have to step out eventually, they found shaded spots outside, and sat down to gossip:

'It's true. She is not dark like us, is she? She is pink like the eastern sky at dusk. Just like a film star.'

'Look at our Maara's fortune. All these years, she was alone on his rock. Now she has a daughter-in-law who looks like a film star. She is going to be busy adoring her.'

'Worried that her daughter-in-law's feet might hurt if they walk on the rock, she will make her tread on cotton. Concerned that her skin might darken in the sun, she will build a palace to keep her safe.'

'Did you see how brilliantly her nose ring shone, catching the sunlight? That must be what knocked Kumaresan down.'

'Hey! Since when do we call him "Kumaresan"? Just because he has found a fair-skinned a girl, have you all renamed our Nōndippayyan?'

'How can we call him Nōndi in front of his new bride?'

'Even if he gets a wife, has children, or even grandchildren, Nōndi will remain Nōndi. Is that going to change? Some of us might know him as Kumaresan, but surely not the entire village?'

From their ceaseless chatter, Saroja gathered that 'Nōndi' was their nickname for Kumaresan. For some reason, she did not like that name. What sort of a name was Nōndi? 'Kumaresan' was such an affectionate name. It was what she preferred to call him.

She recalled how, one afternoon, exhausted from the previous day's work, Kumaresan had been fast asleep on a cot outside his quarters in Tholur. He was not in the habit of sleeping like that, but the tree's alluring shade had cast a spell on him. When she stepped outside her house for some reason, this frozen picture of Kumaresan sleeping under the tree caught her attention. She had stood there looking at him for a while. There was no one else nearby. She walked closer, said, 'Dey! Kumaresa!' and ran back into the house. When she looked out, he was awake and sitting up. She felt bad for having woken him up. She couldn't talk to him right away, but when she got a chance later that evening, she said, 'Did I wake you up?'

He laughed. 'It was you I was talking to in my dream! So after you spoke to me, I cuddled with you and went back to sleep.'

She had smiled shyly.

After that, he'd tell her now and then, 'Please call me "Kumaresa!" just once.' And she would. 'Not like that,' he would say. 'The way you did in my dream the other day.' Then she would soften her voice and call him again. But no matter how many different ways she said his name, he was not satisfied: 'No, it doesn't quite sound the same. Try again.' And if she walked away in a huff, he'd laugh. She had muttered his name in her mind like a chant in so many ways. And here, instead of that lovely name, they called him Nōndi!

Suddenly, like a cloudburst that resumes its torrential downpour after a brief respite, his mother started wailing again.

'Look at him!' she lamented. 'He has brought a girl who cannot even withstand the sun, a girl who faints. What kind of work will she do? Of what use is a girl who does not have the strength to fetch two pots of water? How did he become such an idiot? Is he going to be busy worshipping her with flowers day and night now?' Her voice rose in a dirge:

> I, his mother, had rejoiced that he would bring me an elephant.
> I chirped like a cuckoo that he would bring me a horse.
> I danced in joy like a peacock that he would fetch me a cow.
> I was thrilled that he would bring home a goat.
> But he has unleashed a cat upon us.
> Do I catch and leash it or let it wander free?
> I could not rejoice at the sight
> of a sturdy wedding tent,
> of invited guests, of the sound of drums,
> of him tying the taali.
> That joy, alas, was not mine!

Someone said, 'Please stop it. Whatever it is, our boy has got married. And here you are singing a dirge.' There was mockery in the voice, but it had its effect. His mother's wails were once again reduced to whimpers.

Kumaresan laid down the cot that stood leaning against a wall, and spread a blanket on it. He pulled Saroja up gently and made her lie down on the cot. 'Sleep well. Everything will be all right.'

The commotion outside made her feel even more miserable. She lay like a child on the sagging coir-rope cot. For a second, he wanted to just stay there and look at her. A string of slightly faded flowers lay unfurled.

She was not comfortable on that cot. She was used to lying down on a mat. Bending down, he whispered, 'Forget your tears, and sleep,' and went out.

Her eyes followed him. She didn't know if she could sleep. Lying on the cot inside that thatched hut felt like being trapped alone in a large cave. The incessant babble of voices outside was making her skin crawl. How could she ignore them and sleep? Just as he had pointed out earlier, she had not imagined that so many people lived here.

Since she had only seen a cluster of five or six homesteads from a distance, Saroja had assumed that only a few people would come to see her. She had thought she would manage somehow. Like Kumaresan, she too had made her own plans, but she had not revealed them to him. Neighbours and relatives would definitely come to see the new daughter-in-law. How would she respond to their questions? A smile was always an appropriate response. Then there were words like 'yes' and 'okay'. Until she had properly gauged the people and had a good sense of them, she intended to respond to their queries with just a smile and a few words. She had also picked up some words from Kumaresan's way of talking, which she planned to use at the appropriate time.

But she now realized that none of those tactics would work with this crowd. In fact, it would be best if no one came near her or asked her anything. Anyway, Kumaresan would not allow anyone to talk to her today. But she was afraid that he might go out and pick a fight with someone. So, keeping her ears pricked, she closed her eyes and pretended to be asleep. She could hear them making fun of her fainting, the news of which had reached everyone in the village. 'She must have passed out at the sight of this thatched-hut palace,' they were saying. She lay there, listening to everything.

Earlier, she had seen five or six men in loincloths sitting outside. One of them now said, 'Did you go crazy at the sight of her fair skin, my boy?' She could not hear Kumaresan's response. Perhaps he just smiled, like he did all the time. No matter what situation, his lips always widened in a smile. He could handle everyone with just his smile.

She heard a woman say, 'You are accusing Nōndi, but all you men have wandering eyes.'

The women's chatter had not ended.

Another woman chimed in, 'Since all of you just lie about here in your loincloths, we women aren't worried. If you went out of town to work, who knows what all you'd do?'

'Oh, is that why you don't want to send your husband anywhere?'

'All right,' said one of the men. 'So something happened between the two of you when you were there. That's okay; it's not a mistake. But why didn't you leave her there? You could have gone back once in a while for a few days to enjoy her company. And we could have got you respectably married to a girl from our caste, mapillai. In what way are our women inferior? They may not be as fair as she is, but they are not very dark either.' He said all this without bothering to lower his voice. It made Saroja cry even more.

'Are you asking him to find a fair one and a darker one and ride a double bullock cart?'

'What is wrong with that? Instead of a cart drawn by a single bullock, he could travel in comfort, pulled by two. If he were to twist their tails, they'd carry him around like in a sedan, wouldn't they?'

Even though she could not fully understand the conversation, everything that was being said made Saroja panic. She could sense that they were trying to make Kumaresan reconsider his decision by saying insulting things about her. Could all this talk actually change his mind, she wondered.

She had come placing all her trust in him. What would happen to her? She tried to remind herself of his words to her. The night she walked out of her house, she had been terrified. The day before, she had packed a bag of clothes and given it to him. He had hidden it somewhere. Since his job was to distribute soda bottles to shops, he knew a lot of shops near the bus stop. By the time her older brother came back home it would be past ten at night. Her father, who had returned home drunk and then gone to sleep after eating, had not stirred at all. There was no one to stop her, but she was still gripped by fear. Whenever she looked at her father, she could not control her tears. Nobody from the other houses in their row seemed to be out and about. She heard Kumaresan taking his bicycle out into the street. He would wait for her at the street corner as planned.

She was supposed to leave five minutes after him. Afraid that she would break down while walking past her father sleeping on the cot near the entrance, she hurried out of the house without even turning to look at him. None of the neighbours saw her. Not that it would have mattered even if someone had. When she joined Kumaresan, who was waiting with his bicycle, all that she had bottled up inside broke free, and she wept. Standing beside a thorny bush in a dark spot, he held her tear-streaked face in both his hands and kissed her on her lips. That was his first kiss, and she had felt it with the intensity of a lightning bolt. He had said to her, 'Don't worry about anything. I'll always be by your side.' All her fears had melted away at those words and she sat on the bicycle. That bicycle had brought her to a new life in this foreign land. She could not expect a comforting word here from anyone other than her husband. How would she handle these people in his absence?

Suddenly, for some reason, she was reminded of her brother. Everyone called her 'Saro'; he alone called her 'Roja', a rose. 'I will find you a husband who is willing to live with us in our house,' her brother used to say. 'That way you will always be with us, and if he treats you badly, I can slap him around.' Perhaps, she thought, I should not have left such a brother and run away overnight. She shivered, as though she was coming down with a fever. It would be so much better if Kumaresan came back to her side.

Everyone was asking him about her. When one of them said, 'I don't think people of our caste live in that town,' Kumaresan replied, 'There are one or two people. You would know if you went there.'

'All right. What is her caste?'

'Same as ours.'

'You can't fool us like this, mapillai. There will definitely be a village meeting in a few days. We don't know what the village is going to say. Just be careful. Or . . . like I suggested, take her back and leave her there. You can go once a month and give her some money for expenses.'

'We will see about it, maama,' said Kumaresan.

Would he listen to them? Would he actually take her back and leave her there? She was fine with going back as long as he stayed there with her. Her father and brother wouldn't mind. But would he do it? He had told her that she was the only thing in Tholur he was attached to. 'Had I not met you, I wouldn't have stayed here for so long. You are the reason I have remained in this stinky town.' Hearing that had made her happy then, but now she thought it would have been better if he had liked her town.

She heard one of the men ask Kumaresan, 'How many siblings does she have?' It was only by the voices that she could tell that it was different people talking to him.

'Only one brother.' He explained further, 'She has her father. No mother.' Perhaps he anticipated that their next question would be about her parents.

The same male voice asked, 'What happened to her mother?'

A woman's voice from nearby replied, 'Same story. Who knows whom she ran away with?'

It felt as if something had flown in and hit Saroja on the face. She shrank and buried her face in the blanket. She could hear Kumaresan telling them that her mother had died when Saroja was still a child.

Now another woman said, 'Would she have run away like this if she'd been raised by a woman? She has been raised by a man. That is why she has gone astray like this.'

Saroja was horrified. She had never heard such crude talk before. Her father and brother had never said a rude word to her. Nor had Kumaresan. His talk was smooth, like a banana slipping in castor oil. He was adept at embracing her with his words.

'Just tell us which caste she belongs to,' said an exasperated male voice. 'We can make sure there are no problems.'

'She is from our caste only, maama.'

'Stop saying that. When did our people migrate to those parts? Also, can't we tell by just looking at her?'

'Okay, leave it,' said another voice. 'We will find out eventually.'

She had not expected the people to be so inquisitive about caste here. Kumaresan had told her, 'If they ask about your caste, don't say anything. I will answer.' But for how long could she follow his instructions? What if they asked her in his absence? She had to prepare a plausible response. She had to speak to him about that.

'Where did you get married, mapillai?' a man asked.

'In a temple.'

Kumaresan was determined not to give out too much information. But they were relentless in their questioning.

'Which temple? Where?'

'The Murugan temple in Malayappatti. A hundred weddings happen there every day.'

'Are all of those weddings of the same kind? Of eloping couples?'

He did not reply to that.

'What, mapillai?' someone provoked him. 'Why have you bowed your head? Too scared to look us in the eye and give us an answer?'

Kumaresan had no dearth of courage. He just wanted to be careful about how much he revealed regarding the wedding, where it happened, who all were present. He did not want to give away anything that could cause trouble later. 'Well, one or two of the weddings are like this, maama,' he replied, anger creeping into his voice. 'If all weddings happened this way, would they continue to attract so much attention? Would a crowd like this gather then?' he asked, and walked back into the hut.

Saroja closed her eyes and pretended to be asleep. He unfurled a palm-woven mat on the floor and lay down. She sensed that he was determined not to answer any more questions.

An angry voice grumbled outside, 'Apparently we have all come in throngs to see the temple chariot! A thousand pots have arrived on decorated elephants, and we have come to watch that spectacle. Look! That line of bullock carts stretching up to Kunnoor in the hills. We have come to gawk, he says! Come, everyone. Let's leave. That fair-skinned girl must have spread her legs for Nōndi. Did you hear what he said?'

'We did come to watch, didn't we? When the newly wedded couple arrived, did we come with a plate of arati to welcome them? That's why he said those things.'

'His own mother is singing a funeral song. Look at her, lying like a slain peacock. What would she have said if we had run and welcomed them?'

Finally, one of the men said, 'All right, all right. Leave the couple alone and go mind your business, all of you. We can discuss everything later.'

The crowd dispersed slowly. Kumaresan was exhausted. He tried to sleep. Saroja opened her eyes a little to look at him. Then she closed them again and feigned sleep.

'Wife on the cot, husband on the mat. Isn't this wonderful!' said someone who had, clearly, peeped into the hut.

Saroja had been trembling all this while. She curled up tightly to control her shudders, desperate to lose all sense of place and fall into a deep sleep. But her thoughts did not leave her in peace. She had not imagined that this village would be like this, or that its people would behave this way. She had assumed that people everywhere were like the people in Tholur. Kumaresan had not told her otherwise. She did not even fully understand the way they spoke here, the expressions they used. Their questions did not make complete sense to her.

Kumaresan's hand was the magic carpet that had brought her to a strange land. Perhaps they could have spent a little time in Malayappatti. Why hadn't he thought of that? Why did he trust his people so much? She couldn't help but feel that it was a mistake on her part to have come with him without her father's and brother's knowledge. She had come hoping she would be happy with the man she loved. Her brother had told her that he was planning to marry her to a colleague of his. That's why she had hurried Kumaresan. And as though he had only been waiting for her to ask, he had planned everything in an instant. Perhaps they should have waited a little longer, understood more about what awaited them. These difficulties would not end today. How long would they go on for, she wondered. None of this would have happened if Kumaresan had not gone to Tholur. Why did he?

THREE

Bhai Anna, the man who bought and sold eggs in the area, had stayed at Kumaresan's house one night some time ago.

He came to the village twice a week. If he couldn't finish his work on the day he arrived, he would go to the rock and spend the night in Kumaresan's house. He was happy to stay there, especially if it was the time of the waxing moon. In summer, he never slept inside the hut, but on a cot outside on the rock, gazing at the open sky. This was how he lived. In a different place every day. He was welcome throughout the neighbourhood; wherever he went people offered him a cot to sleep on. Bhai Anna was full of stories. He had roamed around countless towns and villages for many years, and met all sorts of people. How could he not have stories to tell?

Even though he was from Tholur, nothing in his speech betrayed that. Kumaresan's mother often said to him, 'Bhai Anna, you don't feel like a person from another place at all. You are just like one of us in this village. The only difference is that you go down on your knees every now and then to pray to Allah.'

And he agreed. 'After all the time I have spent in your village, even my speech sounds like it belongs here.'

He had his own way of addressing people. All women were 'amma'. And though he knew that the villagers called Kumaresan 'Nōndi', he preferred 'Kumaresa' or 'little brother Kumaresu'. In fact, it was because of Bhai Anna that Kumaresan first went to Tholur.

Apart from the dhoti and shirt that he wore at any given time, Bhai Anna had no other clothes in his possession. If he heard that someone was drawing water from the well in a field somewhere, he would go there, take off his clothes, remove the towel tied around his head, and wear it like a loin cloth. Then he would wash his shirt and underpants that had large pockets to keep money in. After soaking them in the water, he would beat them on the rocks and hang them on a tree to dry. Then he would step down into the canal and have his bath, all the while talking to the man drawing water from the well. Since he was not fond of a quick, crow-like sprinkling of water, he spent a lot time pouring water over himself repeatedly. Watching him scrub away at himself, someone would make fun of him: 'What is this, Bhai Anna? Looks like you have not seen water in months!'

He would laugh. 'I roam around in the sun a lot. If I stay in the water for a while, it cools me down. And this way my clothes also dry in the meantime.' True enough, his clothes were almost dry by the time he was done bathing. And even if they weren't, he wore them anyway, saying, 'They will dry with the heat from my body.' If someone asked him, 'Don't you have another set of clothes, Bhai Anna?' he would say,

'Yes, I do.' But no one knew where he kept them or when he changed into them. But then his white dhoti and shirt, which had turned brown with use, would probably look the same even if he changed regularly.

There was not a soul who hadn't said to him, 'Are you going to build a palace from the money you make selling eggs, Bhai Anna? Why don't you buy some clothes?'

'I have a hard enough time carrying all the work stuff. Why add my own luggage to that?' he would reply.

He carried two wicker baskets. One couldn't find such baskets in these parts. They were round and looked like boxes. They were woven tight with thin wicker strands. When he set them down anywhere, their square bases held them upright. They had a covering of mulch on top, and even had a handle. The mulch covering could be slipped up and down over the handle to open and close the basket, but it could not be removed completely. If the basket was empty, one could dangle it from one's arm. And if it had eggs in it, one could hold it in one's hand. People frequently remarked, 'He carries his basket of eggs like he is carrying a child.' He spread hay inside the basket in several layers, so that the eggs could nestle snugly without knocking against each other. 'If even one breaks, it is not just the egg that is lost, but the very means of my livelihood,' he would say.

Many asked him to buy them such a basket, and he would respond with, 'When I go to my town next, I will get you one.' But so far, he had not brought back a basket for anyone. He never refused such requests outright, and when people reminded him or pressed him further, he simply said, 'But I have not gone home yet.' If they asked, 'Do you mean you have not gone back home in years?' he would reply, 'When I do go, I don't seem to remember about the basket.' At times when he was in good spirits, he'd say, laughing, 'These baskets are specially made and are protected by the chanting of holy words. This is the basis of my whole business. If I buy you such a basket and if you too start wearing it over your shoulders and setting out on business, what will I do? I will lose everything! I will have to spread this towel over my head and sit in a corner somewhere!'

He went from homestead to homestead buying eggs after carefully selecting them. He never tired of walking. As soon as one of his two baskets filled with eggs, he would deposit it safely with someone he knew and set out again to fill the other one. He left the area only once both baskets were filled. Without cramming them in, he could keep up to a hundred and twenty eggs in each basket. If he managed to fill the baskets in two days, his joy knew no bounds. He would then go from Senkundroor to Malayappatti and, by nightfall, have the eggs safely dispatched by bus to Tholur, where they were collected upon arrival. Meanwhile, Bhai Anna would return to the village the same night with his empty baskets.

Sometimes it was midnight by the time he reached the rock, which often prompted Marayi to comment, 'Bhai Anna always comes like a night owl.'

He would spread the contents of his food parcel on the rock, saying, 'If I miss the last bus for the night, I'd have to stay there until the morning. That's why I packed parottas for the way.' And he would offer some to Kumaresan.

Marayi declined to even touch any of it. 'If we get used to the flavours of kurma and kozhambu from restaurants, we will lose our taste for home-cooked food.'

'Marayamma,' Bhai Anna would respond, 'I'd have to starve if I didn't eat food from the shops.'

Kumaresan always ate the parottas with great relish, smacking his lips. Sometimes Bhai Anna would let him eat all of them, and would instead eat the pap from Marayi's kitchen. On days when Marayi made meat, Bhai Anna simply went without food.

Bhai Anna went to Tholur once every two or three months and stayed there for a week or ten days. In the villages where he bought eggs, he'd tell people, 'It will be a week before I return. At least now feed your children some boiled eggs. Don't go selling them elsewhere!'

Everyone liked that. 'This is how a vendor should be,' they said about him. He also made sure no other egg vendor entered this area. Even when he was in Tholur, his thoughts were here.

As far back as Kumaresan could remember, Bhai Anna had been the one buying their eggs. The rock was a great place to raise chickens. They roamed around the entire stretch, laying at least four or five eggs every day. Marayi would store the eggs safely in a salt jar, and by the time Bhai Anna arrived two or three days later, fifteen or twenty eggs would have been collected. He paid four annas per egg. If they had twenty eggs, they could get a lump sum of five rupees. Asking her to fetch a large vessel filled with water, Bhai Anna would drop the eggs one by one into it. He would set aside the eggs that floated right to the top, saying, 'These eggs have gone soft, so cook them today.' The others he would put away safely in his basket.

Marayi became angry once in a while: 'What is this, Bhai Anna? Are we the kind who would cheat you? You test the eggs the way people scratch and test gold.'

But Bhai Anna was not one to be softened by such talk. Nor did he ever get angry. He simply reasoned with her: 'Marayamma, you are a good person. But does the egg care about that? Even if it were a day too old, it would float. I have to take care of my business, don't I?'

One night, when he was lying down outside, Marayi came to him. 'Bhai Anna, you go to all sorts of places. Why don't you help my son find some work? He stays here as though confined within a small measuring cup.'

It had been two years since Kumaresan had completed his eleventh standard. The year he finished school was when a twelfth standard was introduced, but he missed out on it. He always believed that he could have spent another year in school had he been a year younger. Even though he had failed twice, he liked going to school. But when he finished his eleventh standard, Marayi said, 'Enough with this education.' She was not ready to send her only son away for higher studies elsewhere. Besides, she did not have the means to do it.

Kumaresan spent two years in the village doing odd jobs, and sharing some of Marayi's work. But there was nothing he could do on the rock that could bring in more money. Since the goats didn't need more than one person to herd them, he sometimes went with the day labourers to do wage work—digging irrigation channels, drawing water from wells . . . that kind of work. But then someone said to Marayi, 'Those men are not good company. Why do you let him mix with men from other castes? When we offer them water, we pour it without touching them. Yet here is your son, sitting on his haunches and socializing with them, rubbing shoulders with them, and roaming around with them. What can I say? You'll have to find a girl for him from one of *their* families now. After all, who among us would pledge our daughters in marriage to him?'

Rattled by these words, Marayi begged her son, 'Even if all you do is lie here on the cot under the tree, that is enough! You don't have to do wage work with anyone!'

He tried reasoning with her, but his promises to be careful did not sway her one bit. Angry, he spent a few days lying on a cot under the neem tree. She did not ask him anything. She did not even seek his help with work. Finally he got bored and started working in the fields again.

Marayi wanted to find a girl for him to marry. But the first thing prospective families would ask was, 'How much money does the boy have?' It was Marayi's wish to find a daughter-in-law who would come decked with jewellery and accompanied by a bullock cart full of vessels and a rich trousseau. But what did she have that could possibly entice a well-off family? All she owned was the thatched hut on the rock. There were some girls who did seem like a good match, but she found reasons to reject even them. She hoped that her brothers and other relatives would do their part in finding Kumaresan a girl to marry. They did try, but nothing materialized there either. Kumaresan wondered if it was because his uncles were not too keen on deciding anything for fear that they would have to spend on the wedding. If things continued like this, he was not sure he would ever get married. In time, he became convinced that things would happen only if they had money. Growing despondent, he even lost interest in the work around the house.

Marayi related all this to Bhai Anna. He remained silent for a while, before saying, 'Let's see, Marayamma.' When he returned the following week, he had an idea. One of his relatives in Tholur owned four or five soda shops. If Kumaresan went there for a while and gained some experience, he could come back and set up his own shop here. He could easily watch over the field and goats and also run the shop.

'In this day and age,' Bhai Anna said, 'if a man gets used to languishing about in the field like this, nothing will change for him. He'll stay like this forever. It is good to have something else to do.' He evidently knew a lot about shops that sold cold drinks. He continued, 'All he needs to do is to secure business with ten other shops. These days every town has a liquor store; everyone wants soda to go with their alcohol. And then there are Tuesday and Saturday markets where he can sell his soda and cold drinks. He can make a decent living.'

Marayi was reluctant to send her son away for a year. 'Can't you find something for him close by, Bhai Anna?' she asked.

'Marayamma,' came the sage response, 'if I had thought that way for myself, would I be sitting here talking to you? Only if he ventures out will he learn a thing or two and make some money. If you had had a man in the house, you would have somehow done all you could and found a girl for him. The fact that you have raised him all by yourself is a major accomplishment. But now he has sprouted wings. Set him free. Let him fly to a few places and find his own food.'

And so Bhai Anna eventually persuaded her into agreeing. Kumaresan was delighted. Although he liked working the fields, he only had the cattle and his mother for company every single day. The prospect of looking at new faces, meeting new people was thrilling. He had grown tired of swimming around within the confines of his well. He was eager to spread his arms and legs without fear and swim in a vast ocean.

Bhai Anna left earlier than usual the next day mainly because he was taking Kumaresan with him. Marayi packed food for them. The egg vendor laughed. 'Are you still living in the past? Do you think we are going to walk all the way? If we leave before dark and catch the bus, we will be there by morning. And there are plenty of parotta shops on the way.' But Marayi wouldn't listen. So Kumaresan boarded the bus with all the food his mother had lovingly packed.

When he reached Tholur, Kumaresan found that the town was bigger than he had expected. The streets seemed endless, and they all looked similar. Seeing the large cinema halls made him happy. He loved watching movies, but back in the village, getting Marayi's permission to watch even one movie was a tiresome task. 'Do you think we are big landlords who can spend money to watch some dance and song?' she used to say. Here in the town, though, he could watch a movie a week without his mother's nagging.

The man who owned the soda shop was a relative of Bhai Anna's. He owned five such establishments, each in a different part of town. But they were not shops that sold soda. They were actually places—a small room in some narrow gully—where soda was made and bottled. Kumaresan's job was to make the bottled soda and supply batches of it to other small shops that would sell it. For this he was especially given a bicycle. In Tholur these small shops were called 'bunk shops'. It did not make sense to Kumaresan at first. He was only familiar with the two petrol bunks he had seen in Kunnoor. So he assumed that these were shops within petrol bunks. Only later did he learn that it was these small roadside shops that were called 'bunks'. His shop manufactured soda and coloured cold drinks in bottles with round glass stoppers that had to be popped open before drinking. In the shops that sold them, these bottles were kept in small vats filled with water. His job also required him to collect the empty bottles from the shops and fill them with the soda he made.

At one end of town, Kumaresan's employer owned a house that had been divided into several small rented-out portions. Kumaresan operated his soda shop from one of these rooms: a space that contained soda bottles, a machine that made soda, and vats filled with water. It was also where he lived. He even had a kerosene stove which he used to boil jeera to make the coloured drinks, as well as some dishes and pans in which he cooked his food. Although people in the neighbouring sections felt this was their home, Kumaresan did not; he just called it his room.

There was a wide path outside that spanned the entire length of the row of eight rooms. There were some Indian beech trees here and there, in the umbrella-like spread of whose branches Kumaresan found solace. Aside from an allowance for food and other daily expenses, he got a monthly salary of three hundred rupees. He could save the entire amount. Bhai Anna had also given him additional work to do: he had to take the eggs by bus to wherever they needed to go. Since Bhai Anna considered Kumaresan a responsible boy, he had agreed to pay him fifty rupees a month for this additional work.

In the beginning, Kumaresan did not know anything about operating a soda shop. A man by the name of Periyasami came to help him learn the ropes. He was a friendly man of Kumaresan's age, and was from Bommusamuthiram, which was in the same district as Kumaresan's village. The first thing he taught Kumaresan was how to carefully carry the bottles in his hand. Then, for an entire week, Kumaresan was deputed to wash the bottles. Throughout, Periyasami never stopped talking.

'In this row of houses,' he prattled excitedly, 'there are seven or eight girls. Three of them are lovely to look at. You can gaze at them all day long. I have asked Soda Shop Bhai several times to let me work here, but he thinks there is so little to do here that it is enough to let novices handle this place.' When Kumaresan said to him, 'Why don't you find a girl here and get married?' he replied, 'Ayyo! Looking is all I can manage. In fact, I am scared to do even that. And if I do marry a girl here, I can never go back to my village. I'll have to sever all ties with the people of my caste, and live here. If I dare to go back, they will poison me. Or beat me to death.' Fear clenched Periyasami's throat as he said these words, but that did not stop him from resuming his favourite subject: the girls next door.

During his first week, Kumaresan did not know who all lived in the rooms next to him. He always walked with his head bowed. Even back in his village, he had never looked young girls in the eye. Since he lived in a secluded area with his mother, in a house built atop the rock, he did not have many opportunities to meet girls. He only saw them when there was a festival in the temple. At such moments, he was astounded to realize that there were so many girls in his village. But he was too shy to speak to any of them alone. And if he did manage to speak to one, the entire village would know about it the very next minute.

Periyasami and Kumaresan would arrange the bottles in crates and in boxes made of metal wires before setting out on their bicycles. Periyasami would lead the way while Kumaresan followed, lugging two dozen bottles of coloured cold drinks. The idea was to familiarize Kumaresan with the bunk shops he would supply the bottles to as well as the streets he would have to navigate. They did this twice a day, in the morning and the evening. For the rest of the day, Kumaresan stayed cooped up inside the room. A cot stood in a corner of his room, woven with thick ropes which were ripped in places, the frayed strands dangling. During the day, he would drag the cot outside under the shade of the Indian beech tree and recline on it. But he was unable to fall asleep. A person should learn to do nothing, he would think to himself. One day, as he lay tossing and turning on the cot under the tree, his eyes began to close slightly.

That was when he first saw Saroja, shining in the sunlight like a heavenly maiden.

FOUR

A few days after they arrived in Kattuppatti, Saroja sat for a long time in the shade of the neem tree, staring at the winding path that led away from the rock. Kumaresan hadn't returned yet. It was midday, and the sun glowered overhead. Her mother-in-law had gone somewhere, herding the goats. There was no telling when she would return. Hoping that Marayi would say something to her before leaving with the goats, Saroja had walked up to the end of the rock. But the other woman had stayed resolutely silent; she did not even turn to look at her. Saroja had waited alone, standing in the sun's glare. And now she could not recollect how she had found her way to the shade of the neem tree.

The only thing she found comforting about this place was the rock. Her feet were accustomed to plain ground and concrete floors. She had never set her bare feet on a rock before. It touched her with the combined sensation of Kumaresan's soft hands and his rough embrace, the memory of which made her shiver with pleasure every time she walked on the rock's surface. But she had to be cautious. Even a slight stumble and her toenails might get wrenched out, or she might fall face first. Eventually, she got used to walking barefoot on the rock. Like a child learning to walk, she carefully placed one foot in front of another. Then she tried it with her slippers on. It felt like she was constantly alternating between bumps and dips.

She remembered what her mother-in-law had said once while herding the goats away: 'Your flower-soft feet might hurt themselves walking on the rock. Be careful.' But Saroja could not tell if Marayi had been talking to her or to the goats because she had not turned towards her. She must have been speaking to the goats, Saroja concluded. And even if those words were meant for Saroja, it was probably best to think of them as having been intended for the goats. But since then she had not felt like walking on the rock. Instead, she sat a little distance from it, looking at its expanse.

Yesterday, Kumaresan had not gone anywhere. He had to present Saroja to all those who poured in from afar after hearing the news of the marriage. As if to impress upon them that he had not done anything wrong, he laughed and joked with everyone. Throughout, Marayi lay curled up on the cot in the cowshed, refusing to get up. Kumaresan took care of the goats and cows. He did most of the cooking too; Saroja helped. He also made a little bathing enclosure on the rock using old pieces of dried palm leaves held together with sticks and twigs that he gathered from the thorn-covered fences around the fields. He also cut and shaped new palm leaves with the jagged edge of palm fronds, and he wove them into a screen. To her, it seemed like his hands had just woven them by magic. It took him two hours. He kept talking to the visitors while he built it. He did not take anyone's help even to put it up. Yet, suddenly, on a flat spot on the rock, there stood a bathing enclosure. It even had a thatched door. While he worked on it, Saroja had gazed raptly at his hands, at the sheer unpredictability of their movements.

Right after he set up the bathing enclosure, Kumaresan carried a pot to the well and brought back some water. Since the well was quite a distance away, it took a long time to fetch even one pot of water. He then placed a large pitcher inside the makeshift bathroom. The pitcher had a small mouth that led to a large belly. She kept bending down to look into it. 'Be careful, don't get your head caught in it,' he teased. When she set out to fetch some water, he stopped her: 'Soon you will have to do it yourself. But not yet.'

She could understand why he wanted to keep busy and dissolve his energy into work.

One of the visiting women gossiped, 'As soon as he got a wife, he made an enclosure for her to bathe in. All these days he had a mother. *She* never got a private spot like this.'

'Can a mother and wife ever be equal?' retorted another woman.

The women laughed scornfully. Kumaresan did not respond to any of this. But another man spoke on his behalf: 'The girl has come from the city. Do you think she will disrobe and bathe in the wide open like you all do? Doesn't she need some privacy?'

A woman mocked him: 'Yes, all *our* bodies are withered, exposed to the elements. But hers is still golden. Why don't you wrap her around your neck!'

During a brief reprieve from the influx of visitors, Saroja took her first wash in the bathing enclosure made of thatched screens. When she looked up, she could see the sky through the palm trees that leaned over and peered inside. As they swayed in the wind, it appeared as though they were bending and craning their necks to look at her. Two little sparrows observed her for some time and then flew away. She felt shy to even take off her clothes. Still, she somehow washed herself hurriedly and got out. When she returned to the hut, she realized that it was made of thatched palm leaves as well. Something rustled. Every sudden swish frightened her.

How am I going to live here? Will I ever get used to the rock? Will I make friends with the palm trees? Those birds that flew away after looking at me bathing, what must they have thought about me? If I ask Kumaresan about it, he'll probably say something like, 'They must have gone all over the village and said to everyone, "Mohini, the enchantress, is bathing there."' Is that true? Am I truly a celestial Mohini? Is that why they think I've enchanted him?

But she had no time to indulge in such flights of fancy; visitors kept coming.

The same people who laughed and joked outside with Kumaresan changed their demeanour when speaking to Marayi. Once they entered the hut where she was lying down, they spoke as though expressing their condolences. In turn, Marayi talked to the visitors in a low, laboured voice, like someone who had been sick and bedridden for a long time.

'They have come to commiserate, as if some big thing has happened,' Kumaresan said to Saroja, and laughed. Then he whispered in her ear, 'Here, when we say "big thing", we mean a death.'

But she could not enjoy the joke. Her face darkened, and she stared at him. He tapped her chin gently with a forefinger, said, 'Everything will be all right,' and moved away. She could accept that.

That morning, Kumaresan had left after eating. He had told her he wanted to meet some people to discuss the possibilities of setting up a soda shop in the area. A few visitors trickled in after he left. Knowing that this would happen, he had said to her, 'You are an object of wonder for the entire village, not just for me. People might even come in bullock carts from nearby villages just to see you. Don't open your mouth and say anything to any of them. Otherwise they'll surely poke and prod and somehow get all the information from you. We should let this unfolding drama die down before we speak. Only then will we be heard. Be very careful.'

Saroja shuddered every time she heard a voice, and her hands and feet went cold. So she remained inside the hut. Marayi was up from her cot that day, so all the visitors went to see her. She was moving about, murmuring something constantly. To Saroja's ears it sounded just like the rustle of the thatched screens, full of meanings she could not decipher. And precisely for that reason, it filled her with fear. Even when she tried to focus her hearing and listen carefully, the words slipped away from her.

Marayi raved and ranted to the visitors. 'He has brought a hen and kept her hidden in a basket in the hut. Who knows if she'll lay eggs and incubate them, or if they'll all simply rot? I lay here all day yesterday, but no one asked me if I even wanted a drink of water. Still, I have this little stomach to feed. That is why I am up and about today. If death comes to me quickly, then I won't have to witness all these last rites being done to me even while I am alive! The god of death who took away my husband—who knows when he will come for me?'

Some of the visitors gathered right outside the hut where Saroja was, and forced her to step out: 'Hey, girl, come outside. We have come just to see you, haven't we? And there you are, hiding inside Nōndi's loincloth!'

Like a scared little cat, she peered outside the hut and showed them her face. One of the women held Saroja's chin and tilted her face, saying, 'Her face is pale and she looks like someone who is dying of hunger. Is this who Kumaresan has caught and brought here! She doesn't look like she can cook even for two people. In days of harvest, will she be able to do some weeding, or pick grains, or pluck fruits?' The woman went on and on.

Then another woman asked Saroja, 'What is your name, Aaya?'

Saroja took offence to being addressed as 'aaya', as if she was an old woman, but she did not show it. She tersely replied, 'Saroja.'

The woman turned that into a joke: 'Ah! Saroja! Perhaps they named her that because she looks like Sarojadevi, the film star.' Then she added, 'I came to ask you just one thing. May I?'

Saroja looked at her inquiringly.

'How did you bewitch Nōndi?' the woman asked incredulously. 'Some four or five girls here tried to reel him in, but he wouldn't budge. Whenever he saw girls, he would lower his head and walk away. This is a place where men routinely take women who come for wage labour out into the corn field. But Nōndi did not fall for anything. What did you show him that has him so enchanted? How did you talk to him? Where did you meet him? How did you get to know him? Tell me, Aaya. My husband is a ruffian. I ask you so that I too can try to bewitch him. Don't be shy. Tell me, Aaya.'

The woman held Saroja's chin and pretended to plead for advice. She was relentless. Feeling both insulted and annoyed, Saroja quietly slipped away into the hut. After entreating her further, the woman finally left, snidely saying, 'How long can you hide inside the hut? You will have to come out eventually. I will find out from you then.' Saroja could not wait to be rid of her.

Kumaresan had also told her another thing: 'The news must have reached my uncle's place by now. They might come over too. If they do, don't get scared. Just give them a polite word or two in response to whatever they ask.' But by afternoon no one came. Kumaresan too did not return until later.

Saroja had never seen so much variation and play in sunlight before. The harsh sun turned mellow when clouds concealed it, spreading a giant shadow over all the fields for a little while. Then, as the clouds moved away slowly, the sun was back. She kept gazing up at the sky until her neck hurt. She could sense the heat rising from the way her skin tingled and objects began to shimmer in the distance.

She had hoped Kumaresan would return soon, but there was no sign of him. She wondered what was taking him so long. Her eyes stopped at the sun-scorched rock. It just stood there, the colour of dried-up blood. At one spot there was a deep pit, wide enough for one person to lie in comfortably. Apparently, in the rainy season it filled with water. After the month of Panguni, once Chittirai began, it rained in these parts. If they could clean and ready the pit by then, it would fill up with rainwater and they would not have to fetch water from anywhere else for a month. Kumaresan had told her all this the night before. It made her want to walk all over the rock and measure and know everything with her feet.

Suddenly hearing the sound of someone approaching, she turned towards the field. An old woman was walking that way, carrying a basket on her head. Saroja stood up. When she arrived under the shade of the tree, the old woman said, 'Girl, give me a hand with the basket.' Saroja helped her set the basket down. The woman was very dark, as if someone had slathered her all over with eye liner, and her face was beaded with sweat. Heaving a deep sigh of relief, she said, 'I can't carry this basket around from field to field. Girl, can you get me some water?'

Under the cloth covering the basket lay some vegetables. The woman drank the water that Saroja gave her, and said, 'I heard that a new girl has come. You are beautiful. I feel like I might end up casting my evil eye on you.' She gently touched Saroja's face with both her hands and then cracked her knuckles to ward off the evil eye. It made Saroja shy.

'Is your mother-in-law home?' the woman asked her.

Saroja shook her head.

The woman smiled. 'It looks like I will have to pay for you to speak. Is it true that the two of you got married in the month of Panguni? They say that marriages made in Panguni will perish. Panguni weddings are not good for the man's life. Why were you in such a hurry, Aaya?' The old woman paused to observe Saroja's face intently, before carrying on. 'Did our Nōndi boy give you a little something in your womb? Judging by your face, I can tell. You look like a cow mated by the bull three or four months ago.'

It took Saroja a minute to understand the woman's insinuation. The moment she did, her face reddened and she turned away.

'All right, I won't say anything,' continued the old woman. 'Look at me, Aaya. It is just that when I heard it was a Panguni wedding, I was a little doubtful. That is all. When the palm fruit ripens, it will fall on its own anyway.'

The woman was silent for a while, as though lost in thought. Saroja turned to face her. Coming out of her reverie, the old woman said, 'I have some calabash and ridge gourd. Want some?'

But Saroja did not know if she should buy some or not. Understanding her confusion, the woman said, 'Your mother-in-law asked me some time ago to bring these. Here, keep them inside. I will be back in two days. I'll take the money then . . . Now that he is married, Nōndi is the head of the house. Ask him for the money and keep it with you . . . And here, some flowers for you. You are a newly married girl, you should wear them in your hair. I don't want any money for them.' The woman gave her the vegetables and a short string of flowers. Hesitantly, Saroja took them from her and walked into the hut. She placed them on the pot of water inside, and stood there.

Sensing that Saroja wouldn't step out again on her own, the old woman said, 'Come and help me lift the basket on to my head, and then go and lie on the cot. A new bride . . . you may not have slept properly in the night. For some time, Nōndi won't let you sleep; he will torment you and crumple you like anything. Help me with the basket and then go back in, Aaya.'

Saroja was irritated with this idle talk, but she stepped outside to help the woman. Suddenly, the woman touched the chain around Saroja's neck and said, 'Is this gold, dear?'

Saroja just said, 'Hmm.'

'People say that in the towns you now get brass chains that look just like gold. That's why I asked,' said the old woman.

Saroja gently freed the chain from the probing hands of the woman. Something terrified her.

'How many sovereigns?' the woman asked, her shrunken face full of curiosity.

She'll share the information with everyone in the village, thought Saroja. Perhaps I should exaggerate the value of this gold chain. Or will that lead to trouble too? In the end, she didn't reply, but just smiled. The old woman did not know what to make of her smile, and Saroja enjoyed the look of confusion on her face.

But the old granny was not going to leave her at that. 'Come closer,' she said, and pulled Saroja towards her. 'I don't know what caste you are from, but be very careful with these people,' she whispered in a gossipy tone. 'Nōndi has brought you here and set you up alone on this rock. He doesn't have many relatives on his father's side in the vicinity. A distant relative or two might drop by occasionally. Otherwise, nothing much. But relatives on his mother's side are clustered around here like worms. Uncles and granduncles, several of them. They might strangle you to death, and then apply some blue dye on your body and claim that you were bitten by a poisonous snake. You cannot rely on Nōndi. They might wait until he goes somewhere, and then try to chase you away in his absence. They could do anything. Be careful.'

When she looked up at Saroja's face, she saw that it had paled in fear.

'Did you come straight here after the wedding, or did you go and register your marriage with the government first?' she asked.

'We didn't register it,' Saroja muttered in reply.

'Force him to take you with him to get the marriage registered,' the old woman advised Saroja. 'That is the only hold you have. It will scare them into thinking that if they do anything to you, they will have to answer to the government. You have left your people and caste and have come here, placing your trust in him. Who do you have here? None of these dogs will speak for you. You might have caught hold of a strong tamarind branch, as the saying goes, but it is your job to hold on to it tightly, isn't it?'

Saroja could not recollect what the old woman said after that or when exactly she left. Just the idea of going back into the hut terrified her. Involuntarily, her eyes looked up at the roof of the hut. She wondered if it had been a mistake to come all this way, to place her trust in Kumaresan. So far, she had not distrusted Kumaresan even a little bit. But though he was a good man, how could she trust his people?

The time for lunch had passed, but still she could not bring herself to eat anything. As she sat leaning against the neem tree like a statue, the ants that were climbing the tree also wandered on to her body. Fearful thoughts engulfed her. Human faces ambushed her from all directions and fluttered about very close to her. She could not free herself from them, and she curled into herself in disgust. Several hands reached out and scratched her face. She ran about, screaming, blood streaming down her face. Then, abruptly, she was drowning in something. Her imagination kept expanding its range of nightmares.

She sat there for a long while until the sound of a bicycle intruded upon her thoughts. It wasn't Kumaresan. But it was someone his age. The man rode the bicycle straight up to her, as though intent on running into her, and then stopped suddenly, uncomfortably close. The bicycle was rusted, and the seat was torn and in complete disrepair. Though he wore his dhoti around his waist, the loose end of his loincloth could be seen hanging on the outside. A towel encircled his head. He grinned at her, the glint in his eyes suggesting that he wanted to swallow her whole; he was salivating just looking at her. Saroja tried to move away and run back into the hut, but she was trapped.

Still leering at her, he said, 'I am a distant relative of Kumaresan's. I am like his younger brother.'

She did not know how to respond to that. She smiled hesitantly at him.

'I am the grandson of his granduncle,' he continued. 'Look at me carefully. You can see that I resemble your husband,' he said. Saroja couldn't find any likeness. In fact, he didn't even deserve to stand beside Kumaresan. 'The only difference is that he ended up seeing you before I did,' the man muttered, as though talking to himself.

But Saroja understood that she was meant to hear that.

Turning his face eastwards, he added, 'There, do you see a house with a tiled roof and a cowshed? That's our house. If Kumaresan is not here, just call out to me, "Vellapayya!" I will come straight away. You are my older brother's wife. He is a month older than me.'

All this while, he did not get off his bicycle. Trapped between the tree and the bicycle, Saroja hoped he would go away soon.

'They say that I was fair-skinned when I was born,' he continued. 'That's why they named me Vellapayyan. Roaming around in the fields in the sun has made me darker. But I have the same complexion as Kumaresan, perhaps even fairer—a good match to your skin tone.' He looked intently at her face.

Pushing the bicycle's tyre away with her hand, she freed herself and walked towards the hut.

'You are my sister-in-law,' she heard him shout as she entered the hut. 'This brother-in-law is not visiting you now for no reason. I have a message for you from your husband. He has gone somewhere about setting up a shop. He'll be late. I saw him in town. He said, "Go and tell your sister-in-law to get ready. I will come and take her to the movies." So be ready. He will take you to the first show.'

She could not control her tears, but she tried not to make any sound. She could not hear his voice any more. Perhaps he has left, she thought. Yet when she peeped outside, there he was, one foot on the pedal, the other balancing his weight on the ground, his thighs exposed.

He said, 'Get ready to go to the movies. I will join you next time. We can all go together. I have more money than he does. I will give you however much you want. All right. See you.'

She quickly withdrew into the hut. She felt angry with Kumaresan for trusting his message with such a person. But then, had Kumaresan really sent that message? Or was it just this man's excuse to come and look at her? Was that any way to talk to a woman? His grin and the way he had stood, exposing his thigh to her—she was irritated just thinking about it.

She lay curled up on the cot, but she couldn't sleep. The heat reached inside the hut despite the thatched roof. Her mind was not at rest, so she tossed about. She wondered again if Vellapayyan's message was in fact true. Kumaresan liked going to the movies. What if he came expecting her to be ready? He might get angry if she wasn't. The way things stood, she couldn't have him be angry with her too. She could not decide if she should tell him all that had happened that day. If she complained about that white pig, he might get upset and chase away after it, only to get bitten in the end. No, it was best to let some time pass. She would get a better sense of things. The pig would probably visit her frequently, but she would just have to learn to manage that.

Both his talk and his grin reeked of something unpleasant—the stink of some animal rotting within its shrivelled skin. What if he came again during the day, when no one else was around? He might even enter the hut. Today he had stopped his cycle in such a way that she was trapped, unable to move. He might do something like that again. Even if she screamed for help, there was no one nearby. His was the only house in the vicinity. Could she raise her voice to reach beyond that? It would be difficult. Here everyone spoke loudly. And when they were calling someone at a distance, their voices boomed with alarming force. That very morning, Saroja had heard a woman calling out, 'Hey, boy! Hey, boy!' Her voice was such that it must have been heard even two or three miles away. But it didn't seem like a boy had responded.

There was no way Saroja could shout that loudly. She had a shrill voice. Her brother called her his 'sister sparrow'. When they were young, he used to make fun of her voice. He would shriek 'keeeech keeeech' and laugh at her. Conscious of his teasing, she had resolved to speak in a low voice ever since. At times, only she could hear what she was saying. Occasionally, when she had lost her temper and raised her voice, the neighbours had asked, 'Is that really Saroja talking?' Her brother often said, 'She has grown, but her voice is still like a sparrow's.' What could she do now with that voice? How would she handle this man if he came again?

She rose from the cot and got ready. As the day slowly leaned over and fell to the west, her charm as a new bride grew. She combed her hair, wove it into a thick braid, and fixed the flowers the old woman had given her earlier in the day. The arms of her blouse had zari borders and she wore a new sari. She applied some talcum powder on her face, came outside and sat under the tree. She kept staring at the winding path, expecting Kumaresan to return any minute.

She heard her mother-in-law's 'Ho! Ho!' as Marayi herded the goats back home. The animals wandered back and drank water from the tub. Wary of confronting her mother-in-law just then, Saroja turned her face away. The moment Marayi spotted her, she shouted, 'Ayyo!' It was a lament that seemed to tumble out of this crone's mouth all the time: 'Ayyo!'

Saroja stood up in fear. Marayi pointed at her and started her dirge, 'I have one son only—one son to continue my family line. After destroying his life and burying him alive, here she stands on top of his grave, lush like the erukku shrub. I cannot bear to look at this plant! O God! How can I uproot it?' Barely pausing to catch her breath, she continued her tirade, 'At dusk, any good woman would be expected to take the goats in and tether them. She would light the fire to heat water so her husband can have a wash, and stoke the fire in the kitchen to start cooking. That is what a farmer's wife does. But look at *her*! She has decked herself up in all her finery. Only prostitutes stand like this on the streets of Kunnoor town! And my son has brought one of them home! Has she bewitched him by mixing something in his food? How can I release him from her magic? Which doctor can I take him to? How much will I have to spend? Will I ever get my son back, or have I lost him forever to this wretched woman?'

Saroja suddenly felt disgusted at her own appearance. She wanted to tear everything off. In the year that Kumaresan had spent getting to know her, talking to her in a voice dripping with desire, and planning to bring her to the village, he could have given her some idea about how things here would be. She could have asked him to talk about it more. At the time, his words and his affection were all that mattered. Now she wondered if she should have considered her decision more sensibly rather than rely on him alone. But back then, they had been in no state to think carefully about anything.

FIVE

Kumaresan had never looked at any girl surreptitiously, but he could not stop stealing glances at Saroja. He spent very little time actually sleeping under the tree. He simply lay there, hoping for a glimpse of her. Whenever someone approached, he shut his eyes. 'This boy sleeps all the time,' remarked neighbours who walked past him. But Saroja knew that with his eyes half closed and facing her house, he was looking at her.

For him, her every movement—when she walked towards him, when she went away, when she turned this way and that—felt like a whiplash. Yet he bore the pain with pleasure. Even when she was not around, he dreamed of her when he closed his eyes. Once, he saw her carelessly toss her long braid that lay over her chest behind her. All day long, that image had held him in its thrall—its power struck him like a whip falling on a bull's back. Thereafter, each day, there was one such image of her, one gesture, which would haunt him. He even wondered if he should strangle himself with her whip-like braid and die. He was chasing after her even without her knowing. He could not control himself.

Saroja too stole glances at him when he wasn't look-ing. Whenever she went to the leather company where her father and brother worked, men came over to her just to talk to her. But she could not tell one from another. They were all impressed upon her mind as a series of unremark-able, seemingly indistinguishable faces. A composite of a generic man's face with no marked differences. But it was different with Kumaresan. The affection that flowed from his eyes overwhelmed her. She felt that she could drown happily in his eyes. Occasionally, when their eyes met, he was overcome by a shyness that she had never seen in anyone else. It was like the brilliant glow of ashen embers when you blew on them.

She took great care to dress up and make herself beau-tiful so that he would keep looking at her. She dragged out all those new saris that she had stored away in a box for special occasions. Though she had many skirts and long, flowing daavanis, she had tired of them and, instead, wore the few saris she owned. From now on, she told herself, whenever I buy new clothes, they will be saris. Whenever she wore a sari, it reminded her father that she was now of marriageable age. Whenever her brother said, 'Shall we start looking for a boy?' it was Kumaresan's face that appeared in her thoughts. Unlike before, she now spent more time outside. If he was not around, the whole place was filled with her frustration. It did not take her long to realize that the very thought of him engulfed her like a flame. But they still had not exchanged any words.

In time, they began to predict each other's movements. On days when she was at home, he stayed in too. Minutes after she left home carrying her bag, he rode away on his bicycle, fighting the temptation to follow her. He went on his rounds, dropping off cold drink bottles at bunk shops, and then hurried home. He wanted to be there when she came back. Otherwise his heart would sink. If she had returned before him, he would wonder exactly when she had come and by how much time he had missed her arrival. In the afternoons, she did not go anywhere, but Kumaresan had work to do and he left with great reluctance. They knew each other's schedules by heart. Without ever talking to each other, they kept track of the time and made sure they saw one another every day.

Saroja was motherless. He didn't know what had happened to her mother. Later, after getting to know her, when he had asked her about this, she'd merely said, 'She died.' When he asked her how, she said, 'I don't know.' It was not that she was scared he would probe further; she simply did not want to dwell on the subject. So he never brought it up again. She liked that about him. After all, what could she tell him about a mother whose face she didn't even remember? When she had asked her father, she was told, 'She died.' That was all. He didn't reveal anything about how and when.

Kumaresan knew that she had a father and a brother, but he had not seen their faces properly. Both of them worked in a leather factory. They left every day at dawn and by the time they returned it was dark. He could hear the noises they made when they left in the mornings, but he never stepped outside then. He was afraid to show them his face. In fact, he did all he could to make sure they never laid eyes on him. As a result he did not see them either. On Sundays, their one day off, her brother would spread a cot under the tree and sleep soundly, like a corpse. Her father, however, would go out somewhere even on that day. No one knew where.

At night, he could hear them talking. He tried to use their voices to conjure mental images of the two men, but nothing really took shape. Saroja's was the only face that he could hold in his mind. So he tried to make her face more masculine and then derive the other two from it—an older one for her father, and a younger one for her brother. It was not easy for him to imagine a manly version of her. But he thought everything would look like Saroja; he *wanted* everything to look like Saroja. When he told her this much later, she had laughed so hard it brought tears to her eyes. 'No, they both look different,' she told him, and brought two photographs for him to see. They were old photographs, taken when her father was a young man and her brother a little boy. They only muddled the images in his mind even further. Even though he preferred Saroja in her feminine form, in his mind he dressed her up in men's clothes to imagine how her father and brother would look. It was like a game. He enjoyed applying different kinds of makeup on her. His hands touched her face several times during the game. She never complained.

From 9 a.m. onwards, he could hear the notes of Ceylon Radio from Saroja's house. She listened to it while cooking. Even when she was talking to people, she liked to have music playing in the background. Sometimes she would purse her lips and whistle, the sound blending and moving in step with the song.

In his room, Kumaresan too listened to the music from the radio in her house while he worked with the soda bottles. Eventually the song would fade away and only the sound of her whistling would reach his ears and enchant him. Thus, his mind registered every song he heard as a tune that she had whistled. Thereafter, whenever he listened to a song, he closed his eyes and imagined her whistling the tune. The next time he went to the village, he took along a transistor he had bought. It was like taking Saroja with him. From the moment he boarded the bus to when it reached his village, he did not move her from his lap. At times, he clasped her to his chest and dozed off.

Once he was in his village, he could listen to the broadcast from the Trichy radio station clearly and the Kovai broadcast somewhat feebly. His mother was bursting with pride. She placed the transistor on the rock, playing it at full volume, and lay there listening to it. All those who visited her said, 'Look at Marayi's good fortune. She lies about on the rock all day, with the radio next to her. You have to be lucky to get a son like this. Just see what he has bought for his mother.' Kumaresan told his mother a thousand times to keep the transistor safe and Marayi was relieved to know that her son was finally becoming responsible about things.

Before he left, he took the radio in his hand and touched it affectionately. 'What is this!' his mother joked. 'As if you are caressing your wife!' But it made him so shy that he left without turning to look her in the face. She shouted after him, 'Dear! Please don't worry about this radio box. I will take good care of it. I'll even carry it with me when I take the goats out for grazing.' Then she wondered if he would miss the radio while he was away, so she said, 'Please take it with you. Why do I need this?'

'You keep this one,' he replied as he walked away. 'In Tholur we have special radios in which we can also see things, not only listen to them.'

At 8 p.m. on Wednesday nights, the stations broadcast radio plays. Folk from neighbouring fields came to the rock just to listen to them. The place would fill up with people, and even after the broadcast ended they would stay on, chatting. An old woman once came to listen to the play. She said, 'Look at how the man is talking from inside this little box! Maybe he is like the man in the stories, as small as my little finger!' Everyone laughed.

Vellapayyan said, 'Aaya! Aaya! When you yell for your husband, how do people in four other villages hear it?'

'The wind carries my voice,' the old woman replied.

Then Vellapayyan said, 'This is exactly like that. The wind carries so many voices. The radio box pulls them in and releases them to us, see!'

Marayi was happy that the radio brought people to the rock. She felt less bothered by Kumaresan's absence at these times.

Saroja did not like radio plays. Only songs. She knew which broadcast station played songs at what time. Having listened to them all, Kumaresan too knew that by now. At nine in the morning, she would leave, carrying a lunch bag for her father and brother. Two or three other girls would join her from the houses next door. Though it took her a while to return, she was always back in time to listen to the songs that were broadcast after the news at 12:40. Kumaresan waited anxiously for her return. If he heard the songs on the radio, it meant she was nearby.

Within two months, Kumaresan had managed to grasp the work at the soda shop. He prepared and filled the bottles himself, and carried and delivered them to the shops assigned to him. He adjusted his schedule according to Saroja's.

Saroja too had begun to feel drawn towards him. Every day, around seven in the morning, he would stand outside, with only a towel on his bare chest, and clean his teeth with a neem twig. If she stepped out then, her eyes would fall on his back that resembled a dark plank of wood, and she would immediately turn away. All his neighbours found it funny that he used a neem twig. 'Ask your shop owner to buy you a toothbrush!' they teased him. He laughed but never replied to them. He kept his interactions minimal. He also did not step outside unless it was necessary. Even when he looked at Saroja, he made sure there was no third person observing him. She kept hoping he would speak to her on his own, but whenever they were in each other's presence, he became very self-conscious and walked away. She too did not have the courage to initiate a conversation. Four or five months went by thus.

It all changed one afternoon. She had to heat up some milk, otherwise it would go bad. When she picked up the matchbox to light the stove, she found that it was empty. Feeling too lazy to go to the shop at that time of the day, she looked outside to see if anyone was about. Even the old watchman who smoked bidis in between his naps wasn't around. He always had a matchbox next to his pillow. She wouldn't even have had to ask his permission to use it. The doors to some of the houses were shut, while some others were ajar. Everyone must be napping at this hour, she thought.

She could hear sounds from Kumaresan's soda shop. For a while, she stood listening to the rhythmic hiss and grating of the soda machine, punctuated by the peculiar sound made every time a bottle was sealed. Then, gathering her courage, she walked up to his door. He didn't notice her right away. She wondered how to draw his attention. Could she say 'Hey'? Would that be appropriate? He was preoccupied with his work, and it did not look like he was going to turn towards her on his own. She made a feeble attempt at clearing her throat, which no one would have been able to hear, let alone Kumaresan who was sitting so close to the noisy machine. She tried again, clearing her throat more loudly. He turned around, startled. It was bright daylight outside, and dark inside. At first, he could not see anything clearly because of the glare. When his eyes adjusted to the light outside and he saw her, he turned away quickly. Why was she standing there? Had she discovered that he had been surreptitiously looking at her all these months? Had she come to scold him about it?

She hesitated, wondering how to address him. When he realized she was still standing outside, he turned around and walked to the door. His tongue felt dry, stuck to the roof of his mouth. He broke out into a sweat.

'I need a vathichuppullu,' she said, asking for a matchstick.

He was unfamiliar with the term, so he could not understand what she said. Nonetheless, he was eager to give her whatever she wanted. But *what* did she want? Wondering if he had heard her properly, she repeated her request. But he still did not understand her. Was she asking for some cold drink that was available in this town, but one which he clearly did not know about? There were such drinks in Kunnoor. Could that be what she was asking for? He tried hard to figure out what it was she was asking for. She, in turn, wondered if he was playing with her. But it did not seem like he was.

Quickly, she ran to her house and returned with the empty matchbox. He could not help laughing when she showed it to him.

'You need a matchstick?' he said, and quickly went back inside and reappeared with a matchbox.

She took it from him and hurried home. Had she said something wrong? What had she said? He had used another term for 'matchstick'. Did he say 'theekkuchi'? No, he'd said 'neruppukkuchi'. Until then, she had not really heard him speak. She had overheard him chatting with Periyasami, but not very clearly—often it was not possible to distinguish his voice from Periyasami's. Occasionally, she had heard him chase away the dog that tried to huddle close to the cot while he slept under the beech tree, and shoo away crows. If anyone asked him a question, he would reply with a nondescript 'Hmm'. From all that she had a vague sense of how he sounded, and that he had a deep voice. But when he actually spoke to her that day for the first time, she noticed a certain softness within his heavy timbre. Could such a deep voice contain such softness? Now she was too shy to even step outside the house. How would she look at him?

It must have been four in the afternoon. Through the door she had kept ajar, she heard him calling out to her. Now she could recognize his voice. She opened the door wider. She kept her eyes lowered, too shy to look at him directly. But he looked straight at her now and said, 'Vathichuppullu?'

She started laughing uncontrollably. She kept chuckling even after she shut the door. She had never laughed like that ever before.

She had marked that day in her heart. Nothing could match the happiness she felt that day when she spoke to him for the first time. Since then, whenever he wanted to make her laugh, he made an innocent face at her, and said, 'Vathichuppullu'. It made her burst into laughter.

Recalling that moment now, she felt certain that if she stayed with him, that happiness could—and would—last.

SIX

Once their bicycle entered Vairipalayam, Saroja felt a little relieved. The town, unlike Kumaresan's, was full of houses set closer to each other. Most of them had thatched roofs. She looked in wonder at those houses that were wide at the bottom and then slowly tapered towards the top, much like a temple tower. There were some brick houses too. They had the charm of novelty about them. The houses in the interior had tiled roofs. Walking through the town and looking up at the houses that resembled temple towers made her happy. There were only one or two people outside—older people. She couldn't see any women. But it soon occurred to her that the women here, just like Kumaresan's mother, must be the ones who did much of the work in the fields. Here and there, she spotted older women standing, holding on to a goat or a calf. This was not the kind of town where women stayed at home, cooked and waited.

She had heard from her father that they had once lived in a village when she was a child. But she had absolutely no recollection of that time. When she mentioned it, her father said to her, 'It is good in a way that you don't remember any of that. Leave it.' And if she ever brought it up again, he simply said, 'Our town is where we live. All right?' But it looked like her brother had some memories of the village. Whenever she asked him about it, out of curiosity, he told her, 'Here, in this town, you walk about freely, swinging your arms. You can't do that there. Why do we need such a place?' But despite her interest in the village, she had no desire to actually go and see it.

Back in Tholur, in the row of houses they lived in, the neighbours all talked about their hometowns. During festivals they would go away for ten days or even a month. At all those times, they would ask Saroja, 'Aren't you going to your village?' Though it made her sad, she'd just smile and nod. If she had to respond, she would say, 'This is our town. This is where we are from.' For some reason, after moving to Tholur, her father did not ever want to go back to the village. So it was the streets and the people of Tholur who animated her world.

One could walk about swinging one's arms freely on those streets. The town even had a large fort surrounded by a moat, and a large open area full of trees. She had roamed around and played in those places scores of times. When she was a child, her father would take her with him to his place of work. He would leave her to play near the trees within the compound. There were other children her age too. Saroja would join them and lose track of time.

In those days, life was just uninterrupted playtime for her. It was only when her father came to fetch her at lunch-time that she even realized she was hungry. Her brother worked in a different place. His work day ended earlier, so he would come by and collect Saroja, and they would head home together where they cooked dinner before their father arrived. It was her brother who taught Saroja everything. When she came of age, they asked her to stay at home. Although they had lived in different houses in Tholur, all had been in busy, crowded areas. She sighed now, thinking about how she had always lived among throngs of people.

She wondered how her father and brother were managing the food and cooking now. Whether she could cook well or not was immaterial; she had been doing it since the age of ten. On Sundays, if they chose to cook meat, her brother helped her. Her father only did the eating. He knew nothing about preparing meals. He often said, 'Anything blessed with my daughter's touch will taste good.' He never had a complaint about the food she made. Her brother, on the other hand, murmured words of dissatisfaction once in a while, especially when he came home drunk.

That always angered her. 'Go! Go find kurma and kozhambu somewhere else,' she'd shout.

He would retort, 'Oh! Am I not supposed to find fault with anything your majesty does? All that might work on father, but not me.'

Then she would yell, 'You'll get a wife one day. You try all this with her.'

And he would come back with, 'God knows who is unlucky enough to marry you! You shrill creature!'

After a fight like this, they would not talk to each other for two days. It ended only when her brother broke the ice; she was never the one to do so.

On such days, when her father and brother returned home from work, one of them would bring her a packet of savory snack mixture. The sight of that would make all her anger melt away. Whenever her father came home drunk, he was absolutely quiet. His silence was a sign of his drunkenness. With her brother, on the other hand, she'd understand that he was drunk if he came home calling out 'Roja, Roja dear!' from a distance. He would use all sorts of terms of endearment: 'My piece of gold, my little calf . . .'

He was constantly scratching his legs. Sometimes she applied oil on his legs. 'Your legs are full of sores from all the chemicals. Why don't you leave this wretched job?' she scolded him. From foot to knee, his legs were covered with scars of old blisters and new ones forming right on top of them.

'Who else is offering me a job?' he reasoned with her. 'This is the only place that offers work every day. Other than what we spend on our food, all I want is to save some money for your wedding.'

Saroja had never felt the absence of a mother. The only time she thought of her was when someone asked about her.

There weren't too many people out and about in Vairipalayam. But she could hear sounds of children playing. She had not wanted to come here. Or go anywhere really. She had guessed that wherever she went, it would be hotter than it was on the rock back in Kumaresan's village.

There had been one important change over the past week. A cat that had screamed and run away from her when she had first arrived had finally warmed up to her. It came to her, arched its body and rubbed against her legs. If she was lying on the cot, it came and curled up next to her. When she sat down to eat, the cat came and sat close to her, made as if to eat off her plate, and purred. Kumaresan had marked an area of his plate for the cat to eat from. For some reason, Saroja did not like that. How could she eat from the same plate that the cat had just licked?

It didn't matter if she didn't feed it; the cat was still affectionate to her. Once, when she was sleeping, she mistook the cat's gentle touch on her face for Kumaresan's caress. It had come to that. When the cat's tail grazed her, it felt like someone was touching her with a peacock's plume. If she tried to hug it tightly, the cat protested, turning its face to her and expressing its dislike by baring its teeth and hissing. Sometimes, she said, 'All right,' and smiled and let the animal go. At other times, the cat came back to her on its own and tried to settle on her lap. 'You are just like him!' she chided the creature.

The cat was the only other being to accept her. Kumaresan called it 'Kloos'. She tried calling it 'Meow', but it paid her no attention. Then she too started calling it 'Kloos'. Somehow she fell in love with that cat. It didn't stay at home much, and came in only after wandering outside for several hours. She talked to the cat just like she talked to Kumaresan. 'If you leave me alone and go away again, see what I do.' It'd just close its eyes and say, 'Meow'. She'd lift it and place it on her lap.

She thought it would help her days go faster if the cat stayed inside. When she shared this desire with Kumaresan, he said, 'It is a male cat. This is how it will roam around. Soon, it might even go away looking for a female cat.'

She asked him, 'Won't it bring the female cat here?'

He laughed: 'Only humans think like that.'

When she understood his meaning, she blushed.

Since she had come to feel that Kumaresan and the cat were enough company for her, she refused to go out any-where. He had to plead with her for two days before he could persuade her to accompany him on an outing.

There was another reason Saroja did not feel like going out anywhere. A few days earlier she had been ready and waiting for Kumaresan to come and take her to see a film, but her mother-in-law had made a huge ruckus. Saroja had ripped away the flowers she was wearing in her hair, and run back into the hut and flung herself on the cot, sobbing uncontrollably. She lay on a tear-stained pillow, dazed, not knowing if she was asleep or awake. When she became aware of voices and the sound of a bicycle, she slowly came to. It was dark everywhere. She woke up in a panic, feeling as though she was trapped in a cave. When she recognized the voices from outside, she slowly remembered the evening's commotion and started crying again. She could hear her mother-in-law complain to Kumaresan:

'She stood there decked up like a dancing girl. Does a farmer's wife dress up like that? That's why I gave her a scolding. She went back in, crying, and has been lying inside ever since. She has not even lit the lamp yet! I don't know how this house will prosper if she behaves like this. You lost your mind at the sight of her fair skin and brought this ill omen into this house. The only way you will see sense is if you get rid of this harbinger of doom. Otherwise, everything will go to dust, let me tell you.'

Saroja was filled with hatred at how her mother-in-law had completely changed her tone. Earlier, she had likened Saroja to an erukku shrub growing lushly on her son's grave. What does she know about Saroja's state, this plant that has been withering away since coming here? Does she know how lush and healthy this plant was elsewhere? Erukku shrub! Saroja wondered if she would ever forget those words. It was not as if she couldn't think of words with which to retort. But she was putting up with all this because it was Kumaresan's mother. Things would not stay this way forever, surely? And how much longer would this heat last? The rock absorbed all the heat during the day and then let it out at night. One couldn't even step barefoot on it.

She could make out the sounds of Kumaresan parking the bicycle and washing his hands and feet, but she did not hear him entering the hut. Did he walk in like a cat? His breath brushed against her earlobe. 'Have you run out of something? A vathichuppullu, perhaps?' he whispered. But she could not laugh now. His levity only made her cry harder. He lifted her head and placed it on his lap, touching her face gently. She punched his chest with both her hands. He merely leaned back and accepted her punches. Finally, she just fell over and lay on his lap, face down, exhausted. She could do nothing about the copious tears that rolled down her cheeks or her whimpers that were getting louder. The thought that he was all she had left increased her affection for him. Who else could she bare her heart to?

She did not heed his words of consolation. She just kept repeating, 'Let's go back to Tholur. Even if you don't want to live there, at least take me back to my house and leave me there.' If she went back, would her father and brother reject her? Her father would just say, 'What is this you have done?' Her brother wouldn't even ask that much.

She had stayed in a one-room house all these years. The sense of safety that room had given her was not something she could get from this wide open expanse. What could she find here? A ghostly darkness and a violent wind. And all day a heat that singed. How much time could she spend standing in the shade of the tree? She wanted to go back to her house in Tholur, shut and then latch its noisy tin door, and lie curled up on a mat there. That would protect her from everything. The moment she said, 'Take me back and leave me at my place,' Kumaresan touched her lips and stopped her from saying anything further. That warm touch chased away her misery.

'She has not even lit the lamp!' Marayi lashed out from her perch outside the hut. 'And there you are, sitting down to caress and spoil her? Are you acting like a farmer? Nothing I say seems to have any effect. I don't know what black magic she performed on you . . .' She went on muttering angrily to herself in this vein. Perhaps she had expected Kumaresan to go into the hut and scold and hit Saroja for her behaviour. Her litany continued unabated: 'If you spend *all* your time making love to a girl like this, I am sure this thatched hut will become a palace on its own, and a pauper will become a prince.'

But he did not care what his mother was saying. 'We will go to Tholur,' he whispered in Saroja's ears and held her in a tight embrace. 'We have to. Do you think we'll never visit my father-in-law's house?'

After he lit the lamp, it was with great difficulty that he roused her from the cot and made her eat. She had not eaten since morning, but she was not hungry. Though she didn't tell him this, he guessed. He also knew it was because his mother might have spoken cruelly to her. So he kept repeating just one thing to her: 'For a few days, take off your ears and keep them aside. Put them back on only while talking to me . . . Everything will be all right.'

Did he think ears were like necklaces that she could just take off and keep hidden in the holes in the thatched walls of the hut? Her ears were accustomed to the constant hum of human activity, and now, here in this isolated village, they were beginning to yearn for those sounds. In the row of houses back home, there was never a dearth of chatter or noise. Whenever she stepped outside the house, there were always two or three people to ask how she was doing. Sometimes, even if she stayed inside the house, they would call out to her and chat with her. She could hear people talking all the time. But here it was rare to even come across another person. And if she did, it was unlikely that she would hear any affectionate words. In fact, the voices she did hear once in a while pecked away at her like birds of prey feasting on carrion.

The cacophony of crows and mynahs chattering from the palm trees was far more welcome. Birds she had never seen before came to the rock. The clucking of hens kept her company too. The moment they were released from the pen in the mornings, they would shake their feathers about and venture out far into the fields surrounding the rock to find food. It was beautiful to look at them then. Her mother-in-law wouldn't let them linger about in the yard even for a second. She wanted to make sure they got to the field before they started shitting. The hens began their days with a weak, yearning sound and made a variety of noises as the day progressed. Whenever they made a racket, Saroja fervently hoped it was not because of a visitor come to talk to her.

Kumaresan tried to explain why he had sent word through Vellapayyan that afternoon as well as why he could not reach her on time to take her to the film. All that only made her cry more. Kumaresan persevered. 'How long can we manage with the money I saved from the work I did in Tholur? We can't be dependent on amma. If I can set up a shop, everything will be taken care of. Things will take a turn for the better after that. We can even live elsewhere. Please bear with all this until then.'

He did not go anywhere the following day; he stayed back so that he could console her. Once his mother went away herding the goats, he closed the thatched flap which served as a door to the hut, and came and lay beside Saroja on the cot. He tried to comfort her with his body, but her fears, which had vanished in those moments of intimacy, rushed back as soon as it was over, and took hold of her. She kept crying; she had not cried like that ever before.

The day after that, he suggested, 'Let's go out somewhere. Come on.'

She did not want to oblige him immediately. She just wanted to tell him forcefully that she did not want to go anywhere. However, she was afraid he might leave without her, so after a while she agreed and got dressed slowly. She wore a light green sari, but she did not apply anything on her face. At least her mother-in-law wouldn't be able to call her an erukku shrub now. But in truth, it was not the thought of what his mother would say that stopped her from wearing any make-up. She simply did not feel like it. Why should I, she asked herself. Am I getting ready to go and dance in public?

Kumaresan knew the kind of preparations she usually made before leaving the house. The idea of going out always brought her alive like a new bloom. Her entire appearance would shine with freshness. It was enough to make him stop everything and stare at her for a whole day. So her obvious lack of interest right now saddened him.

'What? Is that it?' he asked her pleadingly.

She wanted to say, 'This is enough for an erukku shrub growing in the graveyard,' but she stopped herself. He would have been happier if she had put a little more effort into dressing herself up. No one had found fault with her looks so far. In fact they said things like, 'Look at his good fortune. He has found a girl who sparkles like gold.' It made him beam with pride. She wondered if he was not worried that her plain appearance today might chip away some of that pride.

'Please don't let yourself be affected by the things people say,' he said again. 'You should continue to be the way you have always been. Everything will be all right.'

She did not feel like talking much. 'Hmm,' was all she said.

Her father used to say, 'My daughter's complexion takes after my mother. Who else in our family is so fair-skinned? She is a piece of gold.' After all that had happened, it was her fair skin that seemed to be earning her some respect. She had even begun to doubt if Kumaresan's attentions would have drifted towards her had it not been for her complexion. But the colour of her skin was not going to be enough to survive in this village. She needed a lot more than that. The right caste, more than anything. That is what everyone asked her: 'What is your caste?' Kumaresan had told her very clearly to not say anything about her caste and that he would handle those queries. But now even he struggled in the face of such questions. How much worse would things get?

Even in the row houses back home, her neighbor Mythili akka had been a special case. She wouldn't let anyone inside her house. She would talk to them outside, under the beech tree, and send them away. She distributed the leftovers from her house to others, but never took anything from the others. It took Saroja a long time to understand what was going on. She had heard people say about Mythili akka, 'Does she think she was born superior to us?' But she had initially thought these were personal gripes.

Some time after she got close to Kumaresan, she got the urge to make something special for him. So she asked him, 'Do you like kalakala?' He did not even know what that was. She decided to make it for him anyway. She bought some wheat and sifted it clean. Then she washed the grains, dried them in the sun and ground them into a flour. She could make a lot of snacks with that wheat flour. Eating rice every day was a costly affair. So she would make dosai, kali, chapatti, puris—everything with wheat flour. Even puris she cooked only on occasion, when her brother asked her affectionately, because that required a lot of oil.

She could make many other snacks with wheat flour. Pakodas, made with chickpea flour, would last only a day or two. But kalakala could be stored for up to a month without it going bad. She kneaded the wheat flour, formed it into narrow strips, cut those into small pieces and then fried them in oil. She loved these. Whenever she felt like snacking, she would take a handful of these and munch on them noisily. When she finished making them, she gave Kumaresan a plateful to eat. He loved them too.

'Is this what you called Kala?' he said, deliberately teasing her, because Kala was a female name.

'Not Kala. It is kalakala,' she replied.

'Oh! Two Kalas, is it?' he joked.

She picked up a few pieces and shook them in her hands. It made a sound: kalakalakalakala . . . She said, 'That's the kalakala.'

The snack was so tasty that he couldn't stop eating it. Everything she made was delicious; she could make all sorts of things. The obvious pleasure with which he ate the kalakala made her immensely happy. Since she had made so much, she distributed portions of the snack to each house in the row.

But Mythili akka said, 'What is this? No one in our house will eat this.'

Saroja felt like she'd been slapped.

Another neighbour, Parvati, said to her, 'Don't you know Mythili only accepts things from people of certain castes?'

Until then Saroja had not thought much about caste. She could not believe that there were such people. 'What is her caste?' she inquired.

'It's the caste that boasts so much without any reason to.'

So the other neighbours kept their interactions with Mythili akka and her family to a minimum. But the experience with Mythili akka paled in comparison to the ordeal Saroja was facing here.

Kumaresan had not told Saroja where in Vairipalayam he was taking her. When she asked him all he said was, 'Come with me. You will soon find out.' She did not press him further.

They left after his mother took the goats to graze. Saroja rode with Kumaresan, sitting behind him on his bicycle; she was aware of the prying, inquisitive eyes of those whom they passed. If she heard voices, she thought they were talking about her. She was also afraid that Kumaresan might stop the bicycle to talk to the people who were hailing him. He did reply to their queries but kept pedalling on.

Some people smiled at the young couple. But Saroja did not like those cheerful faces. There was a lot hidden behind those expressions. They insinuated, mockingly, that Saroja was superior to them. For the first time in her life, Saroja was encountering smiles she could not trust.

She heard someone say, 'Look at the bride and groom going together as a couple. I have not seen a sight like this before.' Another voice, a man's, commented, 'Oh, you are going for a film during the day? Nice. Would you have been able to do any of this if you had married within the caste? You are lucky. We are not so fortunate, Nōndi . . .' It felt as though that voice kept following her. She could not bring herself to hold her head high, so she sat with her eyes lowered. It was only after they reached the tarred road that her fears went away.

The shade of the tamarind trees on either side of the road comforted her. At any other time, the sight of these trees—standing so close to each other, blocking the sunlight from reaching the road—would have scared her. But now she was surprised and reassured by it. There was no one else on the road. A canopied road, she thought. One wouldn't find a road like this in Tholur. The trees reached out with their arms from both sides of the road, as though holding her in an embrace. There was a warmth in the gentle breeze, but it still brought respite from all the stuffiness.

She asked him gently, 'Where are you taking me?'

'Tell me where you want to go. I'll take you there.'

'I only want to go back to my house. Take me there and leave me.'

'Did I go through all this trouble just to take you back? Tell me some other place you want to visit.'

'I have come away with you. I will have to go wherever you take me.'

'That's a good girl.'

They came to a steep upward slope on the road. Struggling to make the climb, he hoisted himself above the seat and pedalled forcefully, but he did not ask her to climb down from the bicycle and walk even once.

'Stop,' she said eventually. 'Let us get down and push the bicycle up the slope.'

It seemed he took that as an insult. 'I can do this,' he insisted, putting even more effort into the pedalling. 'If I can't pedal with you on the bicycle, how will I do it later with the weight of the soda bottles?'

But it was a large mound. They had to be patient with it.

'If you don't stop, I will jump,' she finally said.

He stopped without another word.

SEVEN

While they were walking uphill, pushing the bicycle, their sweat-drenched clothes sticking to their backs, he told her where they were going. To his grandfather's place in Vairipalayam. His grandparents—his appucchi and ammayi—were still alive. He had four uncles. And since his mother was the only daughter, they had a special affection for her.

They had married Marayi to Kumaresan's father Velayyan not only because he was known to be a man of good character, but also because he was a hard worker. Also, as he was distantly related to them, they felt that their daughter wouldn't be going too far and they would be able to see her often. Even though Velayyan did not have much land and was not well-to-do even by their standards, they got Marayi married to him. They gave her several pieces of jewellery, and the wedding was a happy affair. For a short while after the ceremony, the couple lived in Velayyan's ancestral house in his village. Then, because they thought they wouldn't be able to manage living out there for long, they moved to the land next to the rock. All told, Velayyan and Marayi led a happily married life.

Whatever little job Marayi needed done, her parents would send someone right away. Whenever they cooked meat or made special snacks, they packed some for Marayi and her husband and sent it in a carrier. When Kumaresan was born, Marayi's parents fussed over him a lot. Until he was one year old, he lived with his mother at his grandparents' home. They even sent food for Velayyan three times a day. And would just any food do for their son-in-law? There was a fresh snack every day, and rice. The entire village said, 'Now that he's got a son, Velayyan gets to eat rice every day!'

They must really have cast their evil eyes on Velayyan because he was not blessed with a long life. He died when Kumaresan was two years old. He always woke up in the mornings the moment he heard the sound of the blackbirds. He had planted chillies inside a large enclosure, and fetched four or five cartloads of compost from Kundroor for it. As a result, the plants had grown huge and lush and taken over the entire space within the enclosure. Velayyan was confident that the plant would yield chillies for two years. He would pick the chillies in the evening, water the plants the following morning, and then carry the harvest to the market. It was a lot of hard work. Between taking care of the child and the chores at home, Marayi too had enough on her hands.

The first thing Velayyan did every day was irrigate the fields with water from the well. Early in the morning the soil around the well was still damp and, therefore, easier for the bulls to tread on without dust rising from the ground. If he started this work late, the ground would have dried and the dust kicked up would choke the animals. He had to run four counts of water for the field and one to be sprinkled on the land around the irrigation mechanism. If he tied the bullocks to the well sweep as early as possible in the day, he could finish the entire task before the heat intensified. The bullocks too did not become exhausted. There was enough water in the well to irrigate two fields. The braided bucket that was sunk low into the well would swell up with water like a pregnant woman and come back up. On one such day, when Velayyan was tying the bullocks to the bamboo poles, they protested and retreated, and Velayyan fell into the well.

No one saw what happened to him. Even today, no one knew what really transpired. It was all speculation. He must have somehow got entangled with the rope, which dragged him backwards, and then he must have fallen through the opening into the depths below. On his way down, he must have knocked into the walls of the well. But he was a strong man; he would have found a way to balance himself. Then how did it happen? He was in the habit of calling out to Marayi once he was done pouring out four buckets of water on to the water channels. She had waited for his call that morning and, upon hearing it, had risen and begun attending to the chores in the house. At that time of the day, he didn't have to yell. He only had to whisper her name, and she'd respond. She was working near the rock when, suddenly, she heard his screams.

When she ran to the well, she saw the bullocks kneeling beside the roller, terrified, with the rope twisted dangerously around their necks. Their eyes were bulging because of the pressure of the rope tightening around their throats. Seeing their eyes shining in the muted early morning light, she screamed. People from the neighbouring fields came running and freed the animals. Velayyan was nowhere to be found. When a few of them peered into the well, they couldn't see anything. They had a hard time keeping Marayi from climbing down into the well. The news reached Vairipalayam and people came rushing. It was only when the sun was high in the sky that they could descend into the well and bring him out. It was his corpse that was fished out. No one could understand what had frightened the bullocks that day. It had never happened before. After all, they had been doing this work for years. What could have thrown them off if not some ghost?

Everyone believed it was the work of some ghost. Then the rumour that one of Velayyan's ancestors had committed suicide at the spot and that his ghost was still wandering in the area began making the rounds. Tongues started wagging: 'He was in too much of a hurry. He thought he'd sell chillies and build a palace with that money. Would this have happened if he had waited until daybreak before he started the irrigation work? We work so hard day and night, but what's the point? Are we going to take it all with us when we die? Everything makes sense only as long as we are alive. Now, see what has happened. He has gone leaving this little boy behind. And she is still a young girl. What will she do? This is why you should keep your ambition in check . . .' People said all sorts of things. They were all jealous of his chilli harvest.

Marayi did not water the chilli plants after that incident, and they dried up slowly. The well too was abandoned; no irrigation was done. Later, when Kumaresan was older, people tried telling him that it might be a good idea to start drawing water from the well again for irrigation. He too tried to convince his mother that doing so might result in better harvests and hence more money. But she was adamant. 'It is enough that we have sacrificed one life. Even if it promises to bring tons of gold, I won't let you do it.'

Marayi's parents asked her to bring Kumaresan and live with them, but she refused. No matter how affectionate people were, she believed that if relationships were to last, it was best to have some distance between the people concerned. Her brothers were married, and their wives now lived with her parents. If she moved in with them, she'd have to put up with the things they might say. She was determined not to go and live with her parents. She had the fields her husband had left for her. Even if all she could get every day was a little bit of gruel, it would be enough. And so she stayed on the rock with little Kumaresan. For several years after her husband died, her father would visit every day after dark and stay at night to keep them company as a protective presence. If there was some work to be done there, he even stayed during the day.

Marayi was only twenty years old at the time. Her parents wanted to make sure that the people of her village didn't get a chance to spread any rumours about her.

Whenever she needed any help, they came rushing. They never let her feel lonely living on the rock in the middle of the farm. None of the other village men could wander around the rock, hoping to take advantage of the young widow. It was only when Kumaresan turned eleven or twelve years old and came to be considered suitable male company that people from her parents' home curbed their frequent visits. Whenever the Mariyamman temple festival happened in Vairipalayam, they all went there in bullock carts and stayed there for a month.

Marayi had told Kumaresan on occasion, 'Your father's relatives didn't ever show their faces here to see how we were doing. I could survive only because my family was so supportive and affectionate towards me. Even my brothers' wives were kind to me. Otherwise, do you think I could have raised you like this?'

His appucchi and uncles started looking for a suitable girl for Kumaresan. He was very dear to all of them, but particularly so to his ammayi. Even if he got into a small argument with his mother, he'd run away to his ammayi's place without telling Marayi. He also spent his school holidays there. Since he was her grandson from her only daughter, his grandmother also spent lavishly on him. But people started saying, 'What's the point in his spending so much time at his uncles'? Are they going to marry one of their daughters to him?'

The daughters of one uncle were all older than him. So marrying any of them was out of the question. The other uncle's daughters were younger than him. He could marry one of them. But his uncles' wives didn't like the idea. They already knew how Marayi's life had turned out after marrying someone from that village. Why risk that again with another girl. But they never said it in so many words; they just said it wasn't a good match. 'We will find an excellent girl for him,' they promised, but it proved to be more difficult than they thought.

Marayi was definitely sad that she could not find a bride from among her own relatives for her son. Sometimes she'd rant and cry, 'Had my husband been alive, had I not been a widow, they would definitely marry their daughter to my son. But now I have become the laughing stock of the village! They think, "What kind of wealth could this wasted woman have amassed?" Why *would* they give us their daughter? Even love and affection need money. If you don't have money, no one will bother with you. Never mind. I will find a girl from some poor family for my son.' Despite her unhappiness, she never spoke ill of her relatives to others. She simply said, 'What can they do if it is not a good match?' She never did anything without consulting her father and brothers first. Whatever money she saved, she gave it to them for safekeeping; even Kumaresan did not know how much of it there was.

By now they would definitely have heard about Kumaresan's marriage to Saroja. On the pretext of herding the goats away for grazing, Marayi must have gone to her parents' place one day and cried her heart out. But until now nobody had come from there to visit the young couple. Kumaresan had thought *someone* would come. He'd expected his appucchi or his uncles to come and scold him and take Marayi with them. He'd thought they'd be relieved to not have to keep looking for a girl for him to marry. But when no one came, he was confused. He wondered if they had cut themselves off, but he was too scared to talk about it with his mother. So he decided to pay them a visit. After all, they wouldn't turn him away if he went there, would they, especially if he was accompanied by his new wife?

He didn't tell his mother where he was going. If he had, she would have complained, 'Now that you have ruined my life here in Kattuppatti and wrecked my reputation in Vairipalayam, why don't you climb the hill in Kunnoor and announce this dishonourable business from there for the whole world to hear?'

She had still not managed to come to terms with the situation. She continued to be in a bad mood and burst into a loud weeping song at every opportunity. So far, she had not said even one affectionate word to Saroja. Or tasted her food. At night, she made some pap for herself and ate it three times a day. When would she calm down and see reason? Would she? Kumaresan had not expected her to be so angry. Perhaps they could have stayed for a while in Malayappatti. Should they not have come here so soon?

When Kumaresan told Saroja that they were going to a relative's place, she was a little scared. He said, 'They love me a lot. They might shout at us. But we can't just sit around here waiting for them to come to us. If we call on them, they can't turn us away, can they?'

'But isn't it a disgrace to visit them uninvited?' she said.

'We don't need an invitation to go to my appucchi's house. It is like our own house,' he laughed. He was afraid she would resist, but she didn't say anything more. She was lost in thought, wondering how she should behave when she met these relatives. She was definitely going to be on exhibition for them. There was nothing more difficult than being the object of everyone's attention and scrutiny. She'd have to sit silently with her head bowed in modesty. At least that way, she would avoid seeing things. But she'd still have to hear the things they said. She consoled herself with the thought that this visit was only a way of hastening the inevitable.

Kumaresan had had good practice pedalling his bicycle with the weight of the soda bottles both in the basket in front and on the carrier at the back. After that one steep incline on the road, Saroja did not have to get off and walk anywhere else. Once he saw her smile, Kumaresan no longer felt her weight on the bicycle.

He stopped the bicycle outside a small, brick, tile-roofed house. That's where his appucchi and ammayi lived. The house was neither within the village nor outside it. Saroja could see four similar houses a little distance away. They had tiled roofs too. All four brothers had built separate houses for themselves on the land that had been divided among them. Kumaresan was telling her all this in a whisper when his grandparents emerged from inside the house.

His appucchi was a tall, well-built man. He rushed towards Kumaresan and slapped him hard, shouting, 'Why have you come here, you shameless dog?'

Wincing under that stinging slap, Kumaresan staggered back, but his appucchi dragged him forward and hit him several times.

'You ungrateful dog!' his appucchi screamed, 'I raised you. I fed you.'

Kumaresan had not expected such a welcome. The bicycle fell down, and he moved aside, holding his hands to his battered cheeks. Saroja, terrified and weeping, hid behind him. Kumaresan appeared shrunk and power-less before his appucchi. His ammayi came running and grabbed her husband's arm before he could hit Kumaresan again.

'How can you hit the boy when he has come to visit us?' she said. 'You may have grown old, but you have no brains. Move aside! Come with me, my dear.' And holding Kumaresan by the hand, she led him into the house.

Though Saroja wanted to leave as soon as possible, she had no choice but to stay with Kumaresan and so she fol-lowed him and his ammayi. His appucchi glared at her. Before Kumaresan could cross the threshold, his appuc-chi shouted from outside, 'Ey! Don't take her inside. Who knows what caste she belongs to! Our eldest son's wife has been keeping a fast so that she can walk the fire pit at the temple festival. This might ruin all that. Let them stay on the veranda.'

Ammayi replied, 'The festival is a month away. Do you think your daughter-in-law has started her fasts already?'

Even so, she led them to the raised platform in the front veranda and sat them down there. Kumaresan was sobbing uncontrollably. Saroja was irritated by his tears, more so because she was not sure if it would be appropriate for her to cry along with him. But she understood his predicament. He had only expected that his relatives would scold them a little. Their response had shocked him, that's why he could not stop crying. She had never seen Kumaresan so upset before. He was always able to handle any situation. Her irritation vanished and she started feeling anxious—she had to rescue them from this situation somehow and leave this place quickly.

His ammayi embraced Kumaresan and said, 'Please don't cry, dear.' Ammayi was so thin that she could easily be snapped in two. Saroja was amazed that she could walk around in that frail body. She had a feeling that ammayi was the only supportive person here, but she would have to wait and see. For all she knew, ammayi was feigning all this apparent concern. Once Kumaresan stopped crying, the older woman rushed into the house and brought out a jug of water. She offered it to Saroja, but then pulled her hand back. She went back inside again and returned with a lead tumbler. Pouring some water into it, she handed the tumbler to Saroja and gave Kumaresan the jug. Hesitantly, Saroja took the tumbler from ammayi and drank the water. It was nowhere near enough to quench her thirst, but she was too afraid to ask for more.

Hearing the commotion, Kumaresan's other relatives had come running from the houses nearby. Saroja did not know any of them, and her husband was in no state to make the introductions.

One of his aunts exclaimed, 'Oh! It is our Nōndi! He has come with his new wife to eat a feast here. Hey, you! Go get the batter ready for some snacks.'

Everyone smiled mockingly at them. They scrutinized Saroja—who sat on the veranda with her head bowed—from all angles.

'Look at her!' said one of the women. 'She was not ashamed to elope with a man, but she is feeling shy now!'

Another one said, 'If the people in Kattuppatti had any regard for their honour, they would have chased this donkey away by now.'

Yet another aunt added, 'Do you know what a great man your father was? In all these years after his death, has anyone dared to say a bad word about your mother? She has preserved this family's honour. You were born in the same family. Yet you stand here after having brought such disgrace upon us. Did you think your uncles have no honour and respect to protect? How dare you come here! At least your appucchi stopped with a few beatings. If your uncles were here, they'd have chopped off your legs!'

Kumaresan did not look at any of them in the face. There were children too in the crowd. These were the same children who used to climb on to his shoulders and for whom he brought gifts whenever he visited from Tholur. They would run and play with him, these same children who now stood away from him, wide-eyed and hesitating. Saroja was relieved that none of his uncles were there that day.

Then appucchi spoke again. 'Run away from here before your uncles return. They want to hack you to pieces. They are very upset that the boy whom they raised has done something like this. Your uncles had plans to build you a tiled house on the rock and get you married to a nice girl. Couldn't you find a girl in our village, from within our caste? We can't even face our people. You have shamed us all. If your uncles see you now, they will hack you to death. Hey, you! Give them something to eat if you want and send them on their way. If our boys ask, we will tell them that we were feeding some workers.'

After that, Saroja did not want to remain there for another minute. She pressed Kumaresan's hand urgently, and he responded by getting up and walking out of appucchi's veranda.

Ammayi said, 'Please wait, my dear. Please eat a little food at least. You have come all the way in the sun.'

One of his uncle's wives snapped, 'Why don't you go with your grandson and cook and clean for him? He has done such a terrible thing. He has forced us all to hang our heads in shame. Do you have to treat him like an esteemed guest?' Kumaresan recognized the voice as it continued its tirade: 'He has brought a woman from somewhere else as if there were no beautiful women in our caste. Who knows? Maybe she brought a lot of gold with her. Maybe he will sell it and build a palace on the rock. People will come and visit him in their cars.' He could not understand how that voice could have lost all the tenderness it used to have. The voice did not relent; instead it gathered in force and venom.

'Look at her, standing in her new sari. She'd probably cast her magic on everyone, this witch! Couldn't she find a man in her own town?'

Contrary to her nature, Saroja broke into a loud sob. Kumaresan held her hand tightly in one of his and lifted the bicycle with the other. He was confused. Have I done everything wrong, he wondered.

EIGHT

It was during the time when Kumaresan hurt his hand that the budding intimacy between him and Saroja finally blossomed.

He had to be very careful while handling the soda bottles that had round glass marbles for stoppers. Even if a small crack formed on the surface of a bottle, it would explode. When he washed the bottles, he had to inspect each one carefully to make sure there were no cracks in it. Kumaresan really liked that task. After he soaked the bottles in a tub for half an hour, all the dirt and grime came off. He would use a bottlebrush to clean the insides and a flat brush to scrub the outside of the bottles. If he sprinkled a little bit of Bassia seed powder on them before washing them, they emerged from the tub sparkling like new. He cleaned all the bottles with great care, as if he was bathing his own children.

Once washed, if he lifted each bottle and held it against the light, he could detect even the tiniest crack. He particularly liked the sheen of the green bottles. Periyasami always teased him, 'Why are you staring at it so intently, like you are looking at a young virgin girl?'

Kumaresan replied, 'You should clean a bottle so thoroughly that you can see through it clearly.'

Periyasami said, 'Oh, you are teaching me now! You have clearly mastered everything! Dey! Don't I know? You think of that skinny, wiry girl when you clean these bottles, don't you? Tell me. With just one look at your face I can tell that you are imagining the shape of her hips as you trace the curve of the glass bottles.'

Periyasami said whatever came to his mind. He always referred to Saroja as 'that skinny, wiry girl'. But it was true that Kumaresan washed the bottles with great care. Unfortunately, he couldn't be that careful all the time.

At the arrack shop, they did not wash the bottles regularly. Whenever it got to the point where one couldn't see the liquid through the dirt encrusted inside the bottle, the crates would come back to Kumaresan's shop for washing. He'd wash them until they sparkled, and the people who brought the crates back from the shop would take soda in those clean bottles as well as in some of the fresh bottles lying around in the shop. When he checked the washed bottles for cracks, there were invariably two or three that he had to discard. He had five or six crates of bottles to wash every week. But he didn't mind, because he liked any work that involved staying in the shop and not going out.

One day Kumaresan was in a hurry. Periyasami did not wash the bottles he had brought back. Instead, those bottles too were filled with soda at the machine and then sealed with the round marble stoppers. Kumaresan carried the bottles outside and placed them in the crates tied to the bicycle.

He had developed a knack of carrying three bottles in each hand, holding them by their necks in the gaps between his fingers. That day he was carrying three in one hand and two in the other.

As he was placing the bottles in one hand in the crate, the ones in his other hand suddenly exploded. Since even just one bottle exploding always set off the others near it, all three bottles in his hand burst at the same time. Kumaresan could not understand what had happened. Periyasami rushed outside. So did the neighbours in the row of houses. Kumaresan stood there with bloodied hands and feet, but he felt no pain yet. He could not even tell who ran where and came back with pieces of cloth to tie bandages on him. It was only when Periyasami was taking him on the bicycle to the hospital that he slowly started to feel the pain. In the three months since he had started working in the soda shop, this was the first mishap that had occurred.

Soda Shop Bhai, the man who owned the soda shop, always told every boy who started working for him, 'Dey! Don't ever underestimate the soda bottle. Why do you think rowdies throw soda bottles whenever there is a riot? Each soda bottle is like a small bomb. If it explodes, you won't know what happened. Each shard of glass will pierce a different part of your body. Always remember that our work is like playing with bombs.'

Kumaresan understood what he'd meant only now. The wound on his right wrist was so big that it needed three sutures. He didn't need any stitches on his legs, but there were gashes in five or six spots. Bhai bore all the expenses for the treatment. Eager that Kumaresan should heal soon, he began sending him biriyani and kari kozhambu from his home once in a while. Kumaresan had not eaten biriyani before. When he mixed the kozhambu and rice together and ate it, he could not believe that anything could be so tasty. The rice was so well-cooked! He devoured the meal without wasting even the smallest grain. Since he had come to Tholur only to make and save money, he was always very careful about how much he spent on food. Whenever Periyasami invited him to eat out, he refused. Now he wondered if getting hurt was a blessing in disguise.

Bhai even suggested Kumaresan go home to his village until his injuries healed fully, but he refused. If his mother saw his wounds, she wouldn't let him return to Tholur. So he told Bhai that he would stay in the shop and keep doing what work he could. Bhai arranged for him to go to a little restaurant not far away and drink some soup every day. It was soup made with the meat and bones from goats' legs. At the shop, they filled a bowl to the brim with the soup. Kumaresan loved it. Periyasami was gladdened by the fact that Kumaresan was sharing his goat-leg soup and biriyani with him. He told him that Bhai paid for it directly.

He said, 'These days, who spends their own money to take care of someone else? Other employers will say, "You weren't careful at work. What can I do about it?" and deduct all the expenses from your salary. But Soda Shop Bhai is not like that. If he was, would you be eating fish and meat like this? If anyone ever gets hurt, Bhai doesn't ignore it. Even I am tempted to wish that the bottles had exploded in my hand instead!'

Kumaresan replied, 'If you want, I can give you a bottle with a crack in it. Fill it up with soda, and take it. It will explode.'

'If the crack is a big one, it will explode right inside the machine. It is only when it is a hairline crack that it takes time to burst. We cannot arrange for that to happen, da!' said Periyasami expertly.

Once in a long while Kumaresan's mother cooked a meaty gravy with goats' legs. Before going to bed at night, she would chop the legs into small pieces, add pepper and other spices, bring the mixture to a boil, douse the fire and put a lid on the vessel. In the morning, she would boil it again. The mixture acquired a slightly burnt smell in the process. Then she would make the gravy with it. The soup he got here had no such burnt smell. When he could get all this here, why did he need to go home? It would take over fifteen days for his wounds to heal and for the sutures to be removed. He would not survive without seeing Saroja for so long. That was the main reason why he refused to take a break and go home to the village.

Thinking back to those days gave Saroja and Kumaresan so much pleasure that their eyes acquired a dreamy, faraway look. Those were the days when they had glowed in the light of their happiness. Periyasami came to the shop every now and then, and Kumaresan sat with him until he filled the bottles and left with them on his rounds. At all other times, he stayed right under the tree that was in the common courtyard. From there, he could see everything Saroja did. He was amazed at how much work she had to do in that one room that was her home. Yet she managed to effortlessly get everything done and also, somehow, communicate with him with her eyes.

The radio was always on. The film *Graamatthu Atthiyaayam*—The Village Chapter—had been released recently. At least one song from the film played on any one of the broadcast channels at least once a day. The song 'Aathu maettula oru paattu kaetkuthu' that Malaysia Vasudevan and S. Janaki had sung became very famous. It came on the radio at least two or three times a day. The moment S. Janaki's voice began with 'Mm . . . gumm gumm . . . mm . . . gumm gumm,' both Kumaresan and Saroja would get excited. Kumaresan would sit up on his cot, turning his gaze now and then towards her house. And, somehow, she made an appearance every time he looked in that direction.

They felt like the song was playing just for them. There was a line in the song about laying a cot in a forest. Whenever he heard that line, Kumaresan would subtly indicate the cot with his eyes, and she would bite her lip shyly and vanish behind the door before timidly reappearing. Towards the end of the song, there was a verse about the hero's raging desire to carry the heroine away with him. Whenever he listened to those lines, Kumaresan's face took on a strange glow and he kept staring at Saroja. He looked away only if something distracted him from his preoccupation. For the two of them, it was as though the song conveyed all that they wanted to tell each other.

Later, when they left Tholur together, she said to him, 'You looked at me *that* way when the line in the song was about stealing the woman away. And now you really are doing it.' And he laughed, saying, 'Yes! I am going to carry you away and lay you on a cot in the forest.'

They had both wanted to watch that film, but they had not even started talking to each other properly then. Besides, Kumaresan's wounds were still healing. He was in no state to go for a movie.

At nine one morning, when she left from home with the lunch bag, she placed a small container outside his door. As she walked away, she kept turning back to glance at him. From inside his room, he saw her and realized that she must have done something special. After waiting until she had walked some distance, he rushed to the door, picked up the vessel and came back into the room. The little pot was filled with kari kozhambu, with pieces of meat floating on top. Every day, he made rice and waited for Periyasami to come and make some kozhambu. Sometimes Periyasami came very late, and on those days, Kumaresan just mixed the rice with some water and drank it.

Leaving the door half-open, he mixed the kozhambu with the rice, and ate it. All her affection was in the kozhambu. He didn't know how she knew that he loved sucking the marrow from the pieces of bone, but she had put two long bones in the kozhambu. He sucked them both with much relish, pleasurably imagining that he was placing his lips on hers and gently sucking on them. How had she managed to get all this meat? Did she go to the market first thing in the morning to buy it? What had she told the vendor? She had given him all the best portions of the meat. She must have picked the meat out herself. Knowing that she had prepared this just for him made him very happy.

He took his time eating. He used his fingers to scoop up every last drop of the kozhambu from the pot, and then licked it clean. The gravy his mother made was very watery, like rasam. He could drink it up. But this kozhambu was different; it was thick and flavourful. Even a small amount was enough to mix with a lot of rice. He wanted to enjoy such pleasures for the rest of his life. When she returned home that afternoon, the little pot with the lid on it was outside her door. She picked it up and went inside. There was a small note inside the sparkling clean vessel. 'I wish for this to last forever. Is that possible?'

Immediately, she said 'Hmm'—a yes—within her heart, but it swelled up slowly and grew into a sound. She thought it would float in the air and reach his ears. She truly believed that he could hear every word she uttered in her heart—that he was aware of all her thoughts, just as she knew his. She tried expressing the 'Hmm' in many different ways. Then, feeling shy, she lay face down on her cot. She could not even think about lunch that day. She fell asleep.

When she woke up, there was the faint murmur of evening everywhere. Guilty at having slept for so long, she went to the bathroom and washed her face. When she stepped out, she ran into Parvati, who smiled at her. Saroja wondered if Parvati knew something. What if she had seen Saroja placing the pot of kozhambu at his door or else him returning the pot later? Saroja did not want to stop and talk to her. She just smiled at Parvati and walked back into the house with her head bowed.

He was not on the cot. And his room was locked. Where could he have gone at this hour, she wondered. But then how long could he lie around on the cot? She knew he went for a little walk in the evenings. What would it be like to join him on these walks, she thought to herself. Kumaresan usually returned in an hour. He would stop at one of the many biriyani shops on the way to get his dinner. Now that he had tasted the biriyani from Bhai's house, he went out to eat biriyani every other day. Bhai had given him extra money, telling him to eat well. When Bhai learned that Kumaresan, his mother's only son, had come from a village to work here, his heart softened towards the young man, and he began giving him a lot of leeway.

That night, Kumaresan did not return at the time he usually did. It had grown dark and lamps were lit every-where. Saroja was anxious about him and could not focus on her work. Perhaps someone from his village had heard about the accident and come to take him back? If that had happened, would he return? Perhaps she could ask the people next door if they knew something. Was that the meaning of Parvati's smile? That Parvati was a shrewd one; she must have observed everything. Was she trying to tell Saroja with her smile that Kumaresan had left? No, it couldn't be. If he was going to leave, he would have somehow given her a sign. She was certain that just as she could not live without seeing him, he too could not survive without seeing her. He must definitely have heard the sound of her 'Hmm'. Even if it had not reached his ears, it would certainly have resounded in his heart. That 'Hmm' would stop him from going away anywhere.

Perhaps Periyasami has taken him to the hospital. Was it time for the sutures to be removed? If that was the case, she wouldn't see him under the tree so much any more. She certainly wanted him to get well soon. But she could not help but wonder how things would be if the sutures were not removed just yet.

NINE

Ever since the debacle at his appucchi's home three days ago, Kumaresan had not spent much time in his hut.

He had finalized an arrangement with a shop that sold soda. It was in Virichipalayam, some distance away from Senkundroor. Being further away, the commute by bicycle was going to be difficult, but he told Saroja that that was the closest decent shop he could find. He would have to collect soda bottles from this particular shop and deliver them to thirteen smaller street-corner shops. Since all the shops were in different villages, it was unlikely that they would run out of soda bottles quickly. This allowed Kumaresan to divide his task between roughly four villages per day. That way, he could visit each shop once in three days.

There were also two weekly fairs where he could deliver soda. And if there was a temple festival going on somewhere, he could get business there too. Some ten or fifteen people had won the right to sell soda and coloured cold drinks on the Senkundroor hill in an auction. If he allied with them, he might be able to sell bottles there next year. In those places, one would have to snare people's attention by yelling,

'Colouraeeee, colour colouraeee!' and 'Sodaaa colouraee! Sodaaa colouraee!' During the Tuesday fairs in Senkundroor, he had seen sellers standing next to their bicycles, carrying bottles and raising their voices in the same way. He could learn to do that too.

The job itself was not a difficult one. It was the preparations that were going to be tiring. First, he had to remove the small carrier on the bicycle and attach a bigger one. Then, on both sides of the carrier, he had to fasten some hooks from which wire boxes could hang. He also needed to fix two hooks on the handlebar of the bicycle so that the boxes he hung there did not slip off. Clearly, he would first have to give the bicycle a much-needed overhaul. This was going to involve a lot of expense and a good deal of running around. But the potential income would be sufficient to provide for their lives here, and he would no longer have to expect his mother to support the household. Once money started coming in, everything would become easier. Had this been Tholur, there would have been ten shops in just one street to which he could deliver bottles. But he could not expect such things here. Not that he was particularly worried about the challenges of setting up a new business. At the moment, his primary concern was that the current commotion should settle down so that peace could prevail.

Though Kumaresan tried not to show it, Saroja knew that he was struggling to raise money for this venture. When he had worked in Tholur, Kumaresan gave all his income to his mother, and though he was certain that she would have kept it all safely, he now hesitated to ask her for help. If Marayi refused, it would be like a slap on the face. In any case, the situation at home was volatile, with her spouting things like, 'If you marry a woman who has nothing to bring, you will soon have to carry an alms bowl and roam the streets. Would any dog worth its salt as much as look at a woman who does not have even a penny to offer?' If he asked her for money now, it would only get worse. So he went to other places to seek help, and returned only by eight or later in the evening after the conch signalling the end of the day's work was blown.

On one such night, he did not even lift his head to look at Saroja. She tried to engage him in conversation, but the only responses she got were distracted, defeated monosyllables. It scared her, because he was all she had. What would she do if he too turned away from her? He had never been this way before. No matter how exhausted he was after a day's work, his face usually broke into a smile as soon as he laid eyes on her. She never had any reason to think that his wellspring of affection for her was beginning to run dry—at least, not yet. Even with the entire village against her, she could keep the spark of her life aflame with the strength he gave her. With just one kiss, he could unburden himself and reassure her. He could carry her in his arms like a piece of cotton, banishing the day's woes. But what had happened to him now?

Not knowing what to do, she spent the following day just like she spent her nights—after sitting under the tree next to the rock, she lay tossing and turning on the cot inside the hut. Having someone drop by just to make fun of her or hurl abuses at her would be preferable to this isolation, she thought restlessly. Even a visit from Vellapayyan would be welcome—anyone, as long as it kept her from worrying about her husband. But there were no visitors that day. It was only when Kumaresan returned at night that Saroja's day dawned. But seeing him so dejected, sitting with his head bowed, his hand reaching distractedly for the food on his plate, she could not help but burst into tears. When he realized why she was crying, he came and sat next to her.

'Don't cry,' he coaxed, bringing his face next to hers.

That was when she smelled the stench. Until that moment, she had never smelled arrack on him. She did not know that he drank alcohol. Was this a new habit? Everything about his place was foreign to her, and now he too was appearing in a new light. What else would she have to see? The thought only made her weep more.

'I was feeling very sad. That's why I drank a little. Only once in a while,' he blabbered incoherently.

She felt as though all her certainties were collapsing. What would happen if things continued like this? Suddenly, she removed the gold chain from around her neck and gave it to him. It was two sovereigns' worth. 'If you need money for the shop,' she said, crying, 'then sell this and use the money. But if you come home drunk, I will die.'

'No, no!' he slurred. 'Keep it . . . keep it. That is all you have left. I won't take that away from you. I will make everything all right. I . . . I won't drink again. Okay? Now, please smile, please.'

And he embraced her. Memories came tumbling over her, and she cried again.

It seemed like her mother-in-law had no desire to get along. She did not expect any affection from Marayi—she wanted only words that did not sting and hurt. Yet every word that Marayi said mauled Saroja's heart. When Kumaresan was away, what did she have to look forward to? Spending her time on a rock that trapped the day's infernal heat, with only her mother-in-law's hurtful barbs for company?

Earlier that day, while sitting in the shade of the tree, Saroja had seen Velayi, from the adjacent field, walk past the rock, carrying an earthen pot.

'Are you going to get some drinking water?' Marayi asked her.

'Yes, athai,' answered Velayi. 'I just came back home herding the goats and saw that there was not a drop of water left. The pot was completely empty.' Then her voice turned angry. 'The planets are against me. All these cursed Saturns in my house, wreaking their vengeance, souring my luck. There has been no respite. If only they would have some consideration for other people's needs.'

'A cursed omen has arrived here too,' Marayi complained. 'All it does is stand under the tree as though possessed, and then it runs to hide inside its burrow. It doesn't even think about helping the house by fetching some water. No. Such basic things shouldn't have to be taught. You just need to be able to learn them yourself.'

Hearing Marayi's conversation with Velayi, Saroja's hand tightened into a fist. She felt like punching her mother-in-law's face. If she had had people here who cared for her, who spoke up for her, would Marayi dare call her a bad omen so openly? Saroja had no one to protect her—that's what gave Marayi the courage to say whatever she wished. Provoked by Marayi's latest slew of insults, Saroja ran into the hut and emerged with a pot. 'Akka, I will go with you,' she told Velayi.

'If a woman carries such a small pot, one meant for children, she won't get enough water to even wash one's feet,' Marayi sniped, looking elsewhere.

But the mud pot was quite heavy. Saroja was not used to carrying a pot on her head, and she didn't know how far she would have to walk with the pot on her hips. So she decided to take the small pot, no matter what Marayi said. Resolute, she looked impassively at Velayi and asked, 'Shall we, Akka?'

Velayi cackled with amazement. 'Look at this! The new girl speaks!'

Saroja immediately recalled Kumaresan's warning not to talk much. She quickly pursed her lips. Once, she was convinced that not talking was going to be the most difficult thing for her to do. After all, she could talk to anyone easily. In the evenings, when her father and brother returned from work, she would chatter non-stop until they said, 'That's enough. Get some sleep now.' But here, in the village, things were different—she was simply afraid to talk. Besides, the fact that she didn't fully understand the way people spoke here, especially if someone spoke very fast, only made things worse. She lived with the constant fear that they would laugh if she said anything.

The well was quite far. To get there, they had to first walk on a path often traversed by bullock carts that sent white dust flying everywhere, and then follow a narrow path that snaked through a harvested field. Velayi had covered her head with the loose end of her sari. Saroja was not used to wearing her sari that way, so her face burned under the sun's glare. It was not until she stood in the shade of the few coconut trees surrounding the well that she felt some respite.

Velayi had talked throughout their arduous walk in the scorching heat. 'How do you pleat your sari in the front?' she queried. 'I have seen women from town doing that. Now all the women here are talking about the front pleats in your sari.'

Only then did Saroja realize that all the women she had seen so far in the village—even the young girls—wore their saris pleated at the back. She had not anticipated that the way she wore her sari would become such a topic of conversation. So she happily offered, 'If you want, I can tie the sari on you that way.'

'Ayyo! No, no!' Velayi replied. 'They'd say, "Look at them both, wearing pleats on the front like prostitutes from the town!" Let some time go by. If you are still here then maybe we could wear our saris that way to some wedding or some other function. And if anyone asks me then, I'll boldly say, "If that girl can wear it like this, why can't I?"' Saroja felt happy, knowing that the women might have some use for her after all.

This was the only good well in town. It was meant to irrigate the fields. Two women were already there, struggling to draw water. One of them stood by a cluster of pots a lit-tle distance away, while the other, with tremendous effort, gripped the bucket that emerged from the depths of the well and carried it to the waiting woman so that the pots could be duly filled. It terrified Saroja to see the women balance themselves, one foot in the shallow canal that bordered the field and the other resting on the elevated ground, as they filled their pots with water.

'Samba,' Velayi addressed the woman carrying the bucket from the well, 'I came here in the hot afternoon to draw water, hoping none of you would be around to bother me.'

'What can we do, Sami?' the woman replied, before walking back to the well with the bucket.

Saroja, who had not spoken much until then, said, 'What is this, Akka? Can't we get water from a tap?'

Everyone laughed. Even the woman who was walking away turned and sniggered at her.

Unable to control her mirth, Velayi said, 'Thank God there aren't any men around!'

The other woman chimed in, 'There is a lot of water in the tap. Open it and see.'

Saroja could not understand *what* she had said that was so wrong, but clearly it was something that had multiple meanings for the others. This is why she stayed quiet most of the time.

Catching her breath between bouts of laughter, Velayi said to the woman, 'Please fill this tap-woman's pot too, Akka.'

Everyone found the joke hilarious, but Saroja's face fell. She felt insulted and did not say a word to Velayi on their way back home. Even though she wanted to find out what she had said that had caused such hilarity, she was afraid to ask. What if it led to further problems? She kept the pot in the hut and lay down on the cot.

Saroja was beginning to feel that her life was like a plant that had been uprooted from where it had flourished and then abruptly transplanted. Would its roots hold on to the earth in this unfamiliar place? Would the soil accept this new plant? Would the plant like the taste of the water here? She was frightened for it. After all, what plant could live and grow on a rock?

She had wanted to speak to Kumaresan about her day, but he was in no state to listen to her. He was so drunk that his neck couldn't seem to support the weight of his head. He did all he could to distract her from his state—he cajoled and begged, but it only made her cry. She did not have the strength to pick a fight with him. She consoled herself with the thought that he had been very resilient so far, and that it was only now that his inner anxieties and struggles were becoming more manifest. If this soda business plan worked out, things would soon be all right. It was only when you had some money in your hand that people respected you. He had some friends in Kundroor who could help him start the business. He often said, 'What would I do if I didn't have these friends?'

Though he tried to hide it from her, Saroja could tell that something in him had come undone after that fateful visit to his grandparents' home. He had expected that his relatives would scold him for his marriage but not actually refuse to help him. He could not believe that they had chased him away. The day they returned from there, Saroja found it impossible to draw him out of his silence. She did not know how to rescue him from the crushing disappointment he was feeling; she did not have words strong enough to do that.

She saw her own assurances failing and crumbling in the face of his troubles while the words that everyone aimed at them continued to land on their targets with great strength and force. Perhaps because she stayed put here on the rock, she was spared the ordeal of encountering too many people. But he roamed around, meeting a lot of people every day. He had no choice but to respond to their invasive queries. To brave their scorn and laughter. Yet, all this while, he had not given her even a hint of these underlying troubles.

But the stench of arrack laid bare the extent of his inner turmoil. She could not tell him anything now. She stopped crying and looked at him. In the light of the lamp, his face was a picture of sadness. She held it tenderly and pulled him close to her chest. It seemed as though he was weeping. Gently caressing his head, she said, 'Don't cry. I am here for you.' Her words gave him something to hold on to. He embraced her tightly, with the fear-filled force of a child who grabs on to his mother, and his whimpers grew louder.

Suddenly, Marayi's voice shattered the peace like the crack of a whip. 'What is this new fascination?' she shouted from outside. 'He goes into the hut as soon as he comes home and shuts the door. He doesn't open it even after the day dawns. Exactly what wonder lies inside that hut? What is this new habit?' Her voice must have travelled the length of at least two or three fields in the dark. She just could not leave them alone in their happiness. She wanted to know everything they said to each other. Even if they whispered inside the hut, she could hear it clearly outside. There could be no secrets here. Even when they spoke very cautiously, they felt like she was standing right outside, listening. During the day, if Kumaresan was at home while Marayi was out, perhaps they could talk then. The nights were unsafe for talking.

When he heard his mother's voice, Kumaresan pulled away from Saroja's embrace, rose, tightened his lungi around his waist, and said, 'Wait. I will be back,' before stepping out.

Did he have to rush to his mother as soon as he heard her voice? What terrible thing would happen if he made her wait for a little while? What could she do? He was always exceedingly polite to his mother. It looked like he was not drunk any more. Saroja sat motionless in the same spot, listening to the conversation unfolding outside.

'What is it, amma?' he asked.

'What do you mean what is it?' snapped Marayi. 'There is a village council meeting today. Someone came and informed me in the afternoon. They are going to start preparations for the festival. They want to talk. Go.'

'Are they waiting for me to go and inaugurate the festival? There are others to do that.'

'You may be a grown man but you are a complete idiot! Do you think they will proceed with the meeting without talking about your affair? They've been patient all this while because they knew this festival meeting was coming up. Today it will only be about your problem. Go and find out what they have to say.'

He considered this for a while. Then he said, 'Whatever it is, we can find out in the morning. If I go now, I might say something that could escalate into an argument.'

'Why would you fight with them? Just answer their questions, tell them what they want to hear. Otherwise they won't leave you in peace. Don't underestimate the village folk. They value their honour. Respect that. That is all I will say.'

'We'll see about all that. You don't worry, Amma,' he said and walked back into the hut.

'Sure! Sure!' Marayi harangued. '*You* don't worry about anything. Just go and bury yourself inside her.'

Not for the first time, Saroja wished she could simply remove her ears, just like Kumaresan often suggested.

TEN

Saroja was always up at dawn. She was used to waking up early to get things ready before her father and brother left for work. Here too, by force of habit, she awoke well before everyone else. Around four in the morning, blackbirds began their clamouring chorus from the palm tree next to the rock, dispelling any chance of sleep for Saroja. Usually, she just lay awake, listening to the sounds of the birds, wondering why they were all aflutter so early in the morning. The sparrows would continue their twittering for a while and then go quiet.

There were no tasks awaiting her upon waking up. Back in Tholur, they had electric lamps. Here, it was quite the effort to light the lantern, which, in any case, emitted far too weak a glow to work in. Yet, it seemed as though her mother-in-law did not need any light; she could work nimbly even in the darkness. Having spent several years on the rock, Marayi knew the place inside out and could find her way around even blindfolded. Saroja could hear Marayi working outside. The goats would soon start bleating. Lying awake on the cot, Saroja let these morning sounds wash over her.

Kumaresan was fast sleep at that hour. She liked looking at him in the light from the hanging lantern. Her mother-in-law's movements came to her as sounds that she had, in her ten days here, learned to distinguish: the faint sound of Marayi fetching water and, a little while later, the splash of water being poured into the pots and pitchers. Saroja had even counted that her mother-in-law fetched about ten or eleven pots of water every day.

The idea of her mother-in-law walking about at dusk, drawing water from that old well and bringing it all the way back terrified her. There was absolutely no light outside. Did Marayi have eyes that could pierce the dark, like some animals did? Just the thought of stepping out in the dark scared Saroja. Even if she carried the lantern, the darkness completely overwhelmed its feeble light. She had been so used to electric lamps that she had never thought that one day she would have to encounter such gloom. Still, if she had to go, she would wake Kumaresan with great effort and ask him to escort her. He would sit outside the hut and wait for her.

The moment they stepped out of the hut, her mother-in-law would pointedly clear her throat. There was no way to know when Marayi slept and when she was awake. At times Saroja wondered if she slept at all. There were so many tasks that had to be done before the first light of the day: fetching water, pouring water for the cows, feeding and milking them. And Marayi did all this singlehandedly.

Whenever she stepped out after sunrise, she would no-tice that the entire place had been swept clean. Initially, she was filled with wonder at how much her mother-in-law managed to get done in the mornings. But now it filled her with dread—though she could not tell what exactly she was scared of. Was it the thought that she too would have to learn to do all of these tasks? Or was it because she wondered if she'd ever be able to brave the dark like a ghost? More than the tasks themselves, perhaps it was her mother-in-law's ability to function with ease in the dark that terrified her? How could she live the rest of her life here in fear? The endless whirl of thoughts exhausted her.

'Are you worried about the village council meeting?' Kumaresan had asked her. 'Let us see what they plan to do,' he added consolingly. 'I have talked to some men my age. They will speak in support of us at the meeting. The villagers won't be able to do much . . . Why are we thinking about all that now?'

He drew her close to him. She liked how he smelled then. Whenever he opened his arms and drew her close, she curled into his embrace. 'You'll fit within the palm of my hand,' he murmured. She was delighted by such talk. All she wanted was to just lie there against him. Nothing more. Why did everyone want to separate them? Often these thoughts encroached upon her mind, unsettling her, and try as she might she couldn't get rid of them easily.

She did not know what time it was when she woke up suddenly, but she was unable to go back to sleep. She wanted to step outside, but she did not have the heart to wake Kumaresan. Lying beside him, she watched him sleep, his body taking up most of the space on the cot. She placed her head on his chest and lay like that for a little while. She had barely closed her eyes when she heard her mother-in-law outside. Every time she tried to close her eyes, they burned with the strain of having wept so much. Yet, she was too scared to venture out on her own. It would be a while before the day dawned properly. Marayi had only fetched four pots of water so far to fill the pitchers in the house. She would definitely do six or seven more rounds. Saroja lay awake, feeling listless.

Suddenly a dog started barking. She realized someone new was approaching their house. It would be good if her mother-in-law returned and dealt with the visitor. Otherwise, she'd have to step outside. What would she tell them? Would Kumaresan wake up now? While she was contemplating all this, she heard a strong male voice boom, 'Shoo! Don't you know a local person from a visitor from outside?'

She turned away from Kumaresan and sat up. Since it was a wide cot, it sank in the middle with the weight of their bodies. She had to raise herself up just as though she was climbing out of a pit. She stood up and arranged her clothes properly before adjusting his, even as he continued to sleep. Otherwise, he might get up and walk outside just as he was. Some nights, he washed himself with warm water while wearing a loincloth, the sight of which made her laugh. He'd wash, change into a different loincloth, and lie down beside her without donning anything over it. Embarrassed, she would tell him, 'Why don't you walk around without that too?' He'd say, 'This is enough for this village.'

She now tucked the loose end of the lungi at his waist and tried to wake him. The sound of her mother-in-law shooing away the dog calmed her down. She sat back down and adjusted her hair. Hearing the voices outside, she could tell that there were at least three visitors. It was about the village council meeting. The dog's barking had completely subsided by then. She tried to listen to the conversation.

Her mother-in-law was saying, 'What is this, maama? You have all come here at this early hour.' Marayi didn't sound like herself; she was anxious about what the village was going to say. Saroja always wondered if her abusive rants and litanies were a way to channel her anxiety. After all, Marayi had never lived anywhere else. She had come to the rock when she was twenty, and had been here ever since, raising her only son. Her morality was her only shield. Perhaps she now feared that her son had compromised it.

A tired voice answered, 'We had to come, Aaya. What your son has done has deprived us of sleep at night.'

Another voice, this time accusatory: 'What if he goes away somewhere once day breaks? It was midnight by the time the meeting ended. Who can sleep at that hour?'

'Please wake up Nōndi and ask him to step outside, Marayi. It is with him that we must speak,' said another man.

'Do you think that wretched dog is going to rise for me?' Marayi wailed. 'Even when things were all right, he had no respect for my yelling. If *she* calls him, I'm certain he'll wake up immediately. I don't have that magic.'

Saroja immediately renewed her efforts to wake Kumaresan up by patting him gently and muttering 'Ttha, ttha!' She finally whispered in his ears, 'People from the village are here. They want to talk to you. Get up. Your mother has started her insults.'

He rose reluctantly and, opening the thatched door, stepped outside. She could hear him saying, 'Welcome, thatha. Welcome, maama.' There was no dearth of these niceties here. People were always ready to say 'Come! Come!' and raise their hands in a friendly gesture. But the same hands were also prepared to hit and chase away the people they did not want around.

Saroja was not sure if she should step outside or not. There was a heaviness in her stomach. For two days now, she had been experiencing some dizziness. In the mornings, she felt weak and dull. She even felt unsteady while walking, and feared that she might fall. She needed to hold on to something at those moments. She had never faced such things before. She decided to wait for him to come back inside. When she focused her attention outside once again, she heard him splashing some water from the pot on his face.

'I painstakingly fetch all this water in the middle of the night,' complained Marayi, 'and you pour it all out without a thought!'

He did not reply to that. In fact, he did not respond to her most of the time. She often scolded him, 'It is like rain on a buffalo. It makes no difference. See!' But he still would not answer.

Some of the men settled on the cot that had been laid down on the rock, others on the large stone nearby. Kumaresan sat in front of them and said, 'Tell me, maama. Why have you come at this hour?'

'It has dawned everywhere, mapillai,' said one of the men. 'It is only you who doesn't seem to notice time flying by.'

Everyone laughed. The door to the hut stood open. Saroja huddled away to make sure they could not see her if they glanced in that direction. From where she sat, she could not really make out their faces clearly, but she could hear them perfectly.

'Mapillai,' began one of the men, 'I don't know what you were thinking when you did what you did. But you are the talk of the entire village today. At the meeting last night, a lot of people said very emphatically that we should not start the preparations for the festival. We don't know what her caste is, they are saying. We don't know where he married her, according to what rituals . . . The point is that he has brought a girl here about whom we know nothing. The entire village bears a mark of impurity if there is a woman here whose caste or family are unknown. And if we start the festival here with this defilement in our midst, we might incur the wrath of Goddess Mariyatha. That's what people are saying. They are saying let's not have the festival at all.'

As soon as he stopped, someone else started. 'Whenever we ask what caste she belongs to, you say she is from our caste only. If that is true, why haven't her parents and relatives come along with the two of you? People are saying, ask him to bring them all here and show us. How do we answer them, mapillai?'

'Only one or two boys your age are speaking in your support,' intoned another voice. 'But even they are not saying anything useful. Only things such as: he liked her, so he married her . . . that has got nothing to do with the village. Do you think this is fair? Tell us. You might have married her elsewhere, but you have brought her *here*. If there is a festival or a function, you will want to take her along with you. Mark my words: All this mixing might work with soda colours, but it doesn't in life.'

Kumaresan, who had stayed quiet until then, suddenly lost his patience. 'I have married her,' he snapped, barely concealing the irritation in his voice. 'What is it that you want me to do now?'

'Do you think you can antagonize the village and remain alive?' came the angry response. The man who said this turned to the others and quipped, 'Why are we even talking to him? Let's just tell him what the village has decided, and leave.'

Kumaresan sat in silence. His mother ranted, 'Would he have done this if he had thought of the welfare of others?'

The man who sounded the oldest among the visitors began speaking in a calm voice. 'Look here, mapillai,' he intoned. 'People said we should stop all preparations for the temple festival. They said we should not start any temple work without getting rid of the impurity that has come to our village because a girl from a different caste is living here. In the end though, everyone agreed that we should not stop preparations just for the sake of one person. But that does not mean we can leave things as they are. If we do that now, then everyone will bring girls from some other caste and keep them here. How can we let that happen? We carry pots of fire and pray to our Mariyatha. Would she tolerate another caste? If something happens to those who carry these firepots, who will take responsibility for that? So what we have decided is . . .'

'Why are you dragging on, maama?' grumbled one of the younger men. 'Why can't you just say it as it is? Look here, mapillai. Until we know which caste the girl is from, we are going to excommunicate your family. We won't take donations for the temple from you, and you will not be welcome at the temple during the festival. No field labourers will come to work at your place. You cannot have any transactions with any of the houses in the village. If you violate these rules, you'll be insulting the village. Let the festival end. After that, we will have you over at the meeting and talk about this again. That's the decision we have arrived at.'

'The girl's parents and relatives should come here,' someone pontificated. 'They should name their caste in front of the entire village. If it turns out that they are from one of our castes, we can figure out what reparations must be made. But if they belong to a caste we cannot mix with, the controls will extend for the rest of your life. Perhaps you could go and live elsewhere. But we can talk about this once the festival is over. In the meantime, think about all this and make your arrangements. Don't try to wriggle out of this by sweet-talking us. The village won't listen. Already, there is some talk in the other villages.'

'Mara, what can you do, you poor thing . . .' a man said. 'This is why we say that we should keep our children here with us no matter what. Once they go out of the village, this is what happens. Even if our boys are all right, do you think the girls in the towns will let them be? Things have not gone too far even now. If he takes her back and leaves her there, everything will be all right. We will think of this a bad dream and forget about it.'

The man was still talking when Marayi began sobbing loudly. 'My whole lineage has been destroyed. What will I do? I went through so much hardship to raise him. Was it all for this? Now if the village pushes us away, what am I to do? I lie on this rock like an orphan. Impose all the controls you want on this dog! But please exclude me from them. Other than the sin of giving birth to him, what have I done? He won't leave her. He enters the hut as soon as he comes back home, and he comes out of it only in the morning. How do you think he'll leave her?'

Her voice must have been audible leagues away. Kumaresan did not say anything. Saroja was once again aware of a strange heaviness in her stomach. Breathless, she felt she had to get out of the hut. She tried to rise, but she couldn't. Her body trembled, and she felt faint.

ELEVEN

Later that day, when Kumaresan was about to set out on business about the shop, Saroja did not let him leave.

Though she didn't fully understand what the village council's decision meant, she was still very scared. She feared that, following that morning's visitors, even more people might arrive unbidden to harangue them. If they did, there was no way she could handle them without Kumaresan around. Even if no one came, the prospect of staying alone was terrifying.

He too was lost in his thoughts. They wanted him to bring all her relatives and present them here before the village. They wanted him to clearly tell them what caste she belonged to. There was no way he could do either of those things. He had naively thought that once they saw Saroja's complexion, they would know she was out of caste but wouldn't bother to probe further. He'd thought there would be talk for a while but it would all settle down eventually.

Perhaps they could live elsewhere. And their land here? What would he do about it? He could leave it all for amma to manage and just go away, taking Saroja with him. But what if these controls and strictures followed them wherever they went in the world? Why couldn't they go back to Tholur? He could keep working for Soda Shop Bhai over there and they could live in one of the rooms in the row? But then what would he do about all the arrangements he had been making to set up a shop here? He would not get the money back now . . . Such thoughts plagued him.

Just a while earlier, soon after sunrise, they had heard the sound of the village crier beating the drum and announcing the village council's decision. Standing at the edge of their rocky field, the man beat the drum four times and then said out loud:

'The meeting about the festival at the Kattuppatti Mari-yaayi temple took place last night. The decision that the village elders have arrived at is that . . . since Kumaresan, son of Velayyan, from the field around the rock, has married and brought a woman from the outside, the village will impose strictures. Therefore, no one from the village should engage in any conversations with them . . . No one should go and work in their fields for weeding or harvest, or call them to work in theirs . . . There should be no exchange of food and water . . . All of this applies to field labourers too . . . These controls will be in place until the Mariyaayi temple festival is over and the village council meets again to reconsider this decision . . .'

Long after sunrise and well into the day, they could hear the crier repeating this announcement in every field and homestead in the village. At first, Saroja was secretly happy that no one from the village would come anywhere near the rock now. But how long could this happiness last? Could they really live here without engaging with people, without transacting with them, looking at their faces, exchanging pleasantries with them? It would be a relief if Kumaresan took her to live elsewhere. Would he refuse to leave the rock and the fields? He might worry about his mother staying alone. They certainly could not take her along. She would much rather roast on this heated rock than go anywhere else. What would he decide then?

Her mother-in-law had started spending more time in the fields. Every time she returned to the rock, she spewed words of abuse that were like burning embers. Since the village's decision had been conveyed, she'd been fuming and ranting even more than usual. She could not bear the sound of the crier's drum resounding all over the place. As long as Kumaresan was at home, she didn't raise her voice much, the force of her litany dwindling to a constant murmur. But the moment he went even a slight distance away from the rock, her voice suddenly gathered strength, making Saroja wonder where she had found this burst of vocal power.

Marayi did not even need a person to talk to. She could speak to the goats, the trees and plants, even while staring into vacant space. Keeping quiet was simply against her nature. Whenever she wanted to communicate with someone not present, she would just imagine them appearing in front of her. Listening to her, it seemed as though these imaginary interlocutors were actually replying to her. Apparently, earlier, she used to talk to Kumaresan's father this way:

'Why have you abandoned me like this? Do you think you will be at peace wherever you are? My curse won't let you be. If I were still married, even if it was to a poor man, at least I could wear a red sari and flowers in my hair, and go to a few places, be treated respectfully. Now wherever I go, because of you, I have to stay in a corner as a widow. What did I ever do to you? Why did you abandon me? What happiness did I experience being married you? And if you *had* to leave, why did you give me a child? Was it because you wanted me to suffer? If I didn't have this one, I would have been back at my father's home, living merrily with my people. You have destroyed that too. You won't be at peace.'

There was not a single day when she did not speak to her husband thus. She had even coined new abuses to hurl at him. 'Dey! Konnavaaya!' That's the name she used most of the time. Kumaresan would say to her, 'Amma, why are you talking to the dead man?' And she would reply, 'Being dead does not mean you have settled your accounts. You are answerable no matter where you are.' Kumaresan had laughed while telling Saroja all this.

'I always imagined,' said Kumaresan, 'that my father appeared in front of my mother and stood there laughing at all that she said. I could never see him. If I tried to picture him, he'd have a crooked mouth, a konnavaayan! That is all. I used to think that if I really remembered his face, perhaps he would appear before my eyes, too.'

But Marayi did not seem to talk much with her husband any more. Only with Kumaresan. If she could chase and hound a dead man, was she going to leave a live one in peace? She didn't say much to him when he was at home, though. Mostly, she stayed silent. Kumaresan said that even that was a way of conversing for her. In his opinion, it was harder to endure this speech of silence. But Saroja could hear Marayi addressing him in his absence. The first few times, she thought Kumaresan had returned and she stepped out of the hut to see if it was so. That's when she realized Marayi often spoke to people who were not there.

Even the way she began these imaginary exchanges was peculiar. She would start talking as if she was chatting with the goat and then slowly turn it into a conversation with Kumaresan. Saroja had to listen carefully to pinpoint exactly when the goat turned into Kumaresan. 'Can't you graze in one place? Do you have to go and graze all over the place? You should live in such a way that people around us respect you. Look at your arrogance! Even after doing something so bad that people want to spit on you, you're walking with your head held high . . .'

All these conversations were about seeking justice for herself. With her husband, she said, 'Is it fair that you have abandoned me like this?' With her son, it was, 'How much I suffered to raise you well! Is *this* how you repay me?' She asked the same thing in several different ways. Sometimes it sounded like she was singing a lament. And each time she recounted some incident from Kumaresan's childhood. It was by listening to these tirades that Saroja learned a lot about his childhood. But she did not fully understand everything her mother-in-law said. In fact, she was completely ignorant of some of the words that Marayi uttered during these outbursts.

One day, Marayi started a story: 'Do you remember what you did one day? Oh, but how would you? You were a little boy who couldn't even wash his own behind. You decided to climb the palm tree and bring down some nungu fruit. The palm tree is challenging even for trained climbers, let alone you—a little boy who was yet to forget the days when he drank his mother's milk. But you somehow managed to climb up to two grown men's height. After that, your hands started trembling and your legs began to sweat. You looked up and felt like you were floating in the sky. And then you just let go and fell to the ground like the fruit of the palm tree. You were unconscious when they brought you here and laid you down on the rock. I heard about it while I was out in the fields with the goats. When I came here, I saw you, my only joy in this world, lying unconscious. There were bruises all over your chest; your body was covered with mud. Thinking you were dead, I took you in my arms and began wailing. That's when you opened your eyes. It was as though the life I had lost was returned to me. Since then, I have never allowed you near a tree, have I? So many people have told me, "A man from our farming community has to learn to climb trees." But I was adamant about it. I decided that I would do all the work, that it was enough if you just helped out. I thought that was enough . . .'

Then her talk would abruptly turn towards the present.

'Who is she? Where is this bitch from? Did she ask you to forget the mother who clasped you to her chest and raised you? If you had any consideration for my feelings, would you have done such a thing? Even though she lived and worked alone, she did so with dignity, this Marayi. Now, because of *you*, she has lost all respect and stands with her head bowed in shame. You have made me the laughing stock of the village. Tell me, is this fair what you have done to me? Is *this* the gratitude you show me for giving birth to you and bringing you up? This body that held you in it is now burning with the fire of injustice. How will I put out that fire now?'

As she spat out those last words, she untied her hair and beat her chest violently. Listening to such an outburst instilled a cold fear in Saroja's heart, and she stayed huddled inside the hut without so much as peeping out. She feared that if she stepped outside, Marayi's words, swirling about like a ghostly storm, might sweep her away.

When she mentioned this to Kumaresan at night, he'd say, 'Poor amma, what can she do? Whom can she tell her woes to? Let her talk. After all, it is only me she is talking about.'

Saroja wanted to tell him, 'It is not only you that she talks about. She talks about me too.' But she controlled herself. Marayi did not launch into her histrionics when Kumaresan was around. Saroja often hoped that her mother-in-law would vent her spleen in front of him, just so that he could hear it himself. Now, with this new development concerning the village council's decision, she was terrified

140

of what Marayi's ire would unleash, and begged Kumaresan to stay at home. He told her that if he went and got some things done today, he might have the shop ready in a few days. Despite that, she insisted that he stay with her.

Meanwhile, her mother-in-law went about her work, muttering bitterly to herself. Before she left with the goats, Marayi drank some water from the pot. 'From today onwards,' she moaned, 'we won't get even this water. They won't even let us go near the well. We will just have to drink the salty water we get here and stay thirsty. But why should I expect this thirst to be quenched? After all, which of my desires has been fulfilled in this life? Never mind . . .' The goats tried to spread out in different directions. 'You will have respect as long as you stay with the crowd. You will lose it as soon as you start going your way,' she shouted to the goats and ran after them. Her words echoed over the rock and lingered there.

That day, even Saroja and Kumaresan were at a loss for what to say to each other. No one ventured near the rock. Even those who habitually walked past the rock to get to the other side took roundabout detours instead. Usually, even if they were walking some distance away, the villagers would stop to exchange a few words in greeting. But none of that happened that day. Saroja began to understand that being prohibited from going to the village was a serious thing. All they heard were the sounds of birds now and then.

'What should we do now?' she asked him.

'We'll see.'

She realized that he had not made any decisions.

'Who knows what they will do if they find out what caste I am from?' she said, fearfully. 'Please take me back home and leave me there.'

'That's the only thing I do not want to hear. I married you. I will not abandon you,' he said, looking intently at her. There was no dishonesty in his words.

Once in a while, they heard the crows cawing from their perches on the palm tree. Now and then, they exchanged a few perfunctory words. They ate without even tasting the food, and sat restlessly inside the hut in the afternoon. Suddenly, they heard a voice calling out, 'Dey! Nōndippayya, Nōndippayya!'

Surprised by that voice, they both rushed outside to see who it was.

'If it is so hot already in Panguni, who knows how much worse it will get in Chittirai?' said a middle-aged woman standing outside the hut. 'When men go astray, even the sky gets angry. Not a drop of rain.' The woman covered her head with the end of her sari, protecting it from the sun. Saroja realized that there were still people in the village she had not yet met.

Kumaresan welcomed her: 'Come, Akka! Chellakka, come!'

She sat down under the neem tree, sighing, 'Oh God, how hot it is!'

'Saroja, bring some water,' said Kumaresan.

'No, boy,' said the woman. 'I just drank some in the field.'

In her faded sari, she looked like a field labourer. Here, there was no practice of inviting the workers into the house. They could sit anywhere on the rock. Mostly, they sat under the neem tree. If they had to stay the night, they'd spread a cot on the rock.

'Tomorrow,' continued the woman, 'we are conducting a coming-of-age ceremony for my daughter. I am here to invite you for that. For ten days now, it has all been about your problem. I didn't want to come to this village. My husband and I fought over whether we should invite you or not. Yesterday, he finally relented. "Even poor and destitute people come here," he said. "They come carrying their bundles of clothes. I will think of them that way. Go and invite them." That's why I am here today. Both of you—husband and wife—please do come. I already saw your mother on the pasture and informed her. Please don't worry about anything, Nōndi. You are going through a bad time—that's why you are getting into all these unnecessary problems. What can you do if it is written in your fate that you need to stand in shame in front of people? I know about the village council's decisions and prohibitions. But they don't apply to our village. I want both of you to come in the evening, stay for the entire function, and leave only after you eat at the dinner feast. You are like a maternal uncle to my daughter. No matter what you have done, I cannot bear the idea of conducting the ceremony without your blessings, Nōndi. Hey, girl! Don't think I haven't invited you. You come too.' And then the woman left.

Once she was gone, Kumaresan told Saroja about her—she was a distant relative, an elder sister of sorts. Her parents had married her to someone in Molappalayam, which was two villages away. 'When I was a child, I had great affection for her. She too was very fond of me. See! She even fought with her husband for me!' he added proudly.

'Is that why she is rushing away without so much as drinking water here?' said Saroja.

He did not reply to that.

'Shall we go tomorrow?' she asked him.

'Of course!' he said 'How can we not go after she has come all this way to invite us? She specifically invited you too. Let us both go.'

Saroja then gently voiced the doubt gnawing away at her: 'Her lips certainly invited me. But I think her heart didn't want me.'

'You are afraid of everything!' he burst out angrily. 'Only if we start going to a few places will people begin respecting us. *Accepting* us. If we just hide here, we will be alone forever.'

Saroja did not respond, but fear settled in her heart like a rock, firm and unshakeable.

TWELVE

Three large, hilly mounds impeded their journey to Virichipalayam.

Saroja insisted Kumaresan stop the bicycle. So they walked, pushing the bicycle along. The night before, she had convinced him to take her with him to see the new shop. Saroja had woken up as soon as she heard her mother-in-law moving about, and quickly finished cooking. The thought that she was going to be out with Kumaresan had helped her conquer her fear of working in the dark. She packed food for the morning and the afternoon in separate containers.

In Tholur, she had carried lunch for her father and brother in separate metal boxes with tight lids to ensure the sambar or rasam inside did not spill out. You could get different kinds of bags there as well. She had two wide bags woven with a thin but sturdy wire that she had picked out herself. They made the task of carrying food a joyful prospect. She could fit all the lunch boxes into those bags, as well as the plates and ladles, and use a towel to cover the top. When those bags were new, she had felt a strange pride in carrying them. Even though she had to switch hands periodically to balance the weight, she never grew tired of holding them. But here, in the village, there were no such bags, no such boxes. Most of the vessels were earthen. She had a hard time memorizing their names. Initially, when Kumaresan said, 'Sochatti, saachatti,' she had no idea what he was talking about. Then he explained it to her. Sochatti was sotthu-chatti, the vessel in which rice or any other grain was cooked. Saachatti was saaru-chatti, in which gravies were prepared. He often spoke to her as if she too was from Kattuppatti. Everyone did. But it was particularly disorienting when Kumaresan did it.

When she got upset with him for speaking to her that way, he started explaining everything to her patiently. She learned the difference between melolachatti, thadachatti, peraalachatti, neechatti, mutti and soppu. It took time to get used to cooking in those vessels, so she was very careful with them. After all, if any of them broke, she would be held accountable. Many of these earthen pots had turned black at the bottom from resting repeatedly over a flame. Kumaresan told her that she should not press them too hard while washing them. There were a few lead vessels—some plates and tumblers. There were no other metal utensils. Apparently, the silver and brass utensils his mother received as wedding gifts still lay in the loft in his appucchi's house.

'Do I have a lot of children here to use all the silver and brass stuff?' Marayi used to say to anyone who asked. 'I am all alone. Mud vessels will do. When he brings a wife, let her start using all the utensils. He will build her a house, won't he?' But this daughter-in-law was certainly not going to get to use all those silver and brass vessels.

'They might even say they won't give us all that stuff any more,' Kumaresan had once told Saroja. 'But amma won't let that go so easily.'

The lunch carrier he had taken to school and another brass vessel lay inside the large pot in a corner of the hut. That morning, Saroja had taken them out and washed them. They were the only vessels that had tightly fitting lids. For the other vessels, she covered them with plates and tied pieces of cloth securely around them. Kumaresan had recently bought a khaki bag. She now packed everything inside that bag. It was only after she was done with everything that she woke him up.

What if he changes his mind in the morning and refuses to take me along, she had wondered. Since she didn't want to risk that possibility, she had decided to finish all the work and get ready before he awoke.

While filling the pots with water, Marayi had seen Saroja doing all the cooking. She even sang a song that made fun of a girl who packed food with the hope of going somewhere by bullock cart. But Saroja ignored her.

When Kumaresan was ready to leave, he said, 'Amma, I am going to the shop.'

Marayi snapped, 'The last time you went away to work, you brought ruin upon our heads. Who knows what you will bring this time? You have made sure no one talks to us again. All that is left now is the life in this body. Take that too and leave here for good!'

Kumaresan did not say anything to that. He hung the food bags from the handlebars of the bicycle. Had he already affixed the hooks for carrying soda bottles, they would have come in handy now. Instead, the bags kept sliding down the handlebars. If he hung them both together, the vessels might jostle and clash inside, possibly spilling their contents. So Saroja asked him not to hang them on the handlebars. Taking them from him, she kept them on her lap.

This was the first time she was going out with him after that fateful visit to appucchi's house. She shuddered at the memory. But now they were not going to a relative's house. They were going to a new village where no one knew who she was. In the tender heat of that morning, she was very excited to go out with him. It had not been easy for her convince him to let her go with him. He had one condition.

'All right. I will take you with me. But once we are back, we should both go to Chellakka's house for the ceremony. You should definitely come with me. If you agree to that, I will take you with me in the morning.'

She consented without even thinking about it. All she wanted was to be away from the rock for a day. The rock had no compassion for her. Only on those nights when Kumaresan was next to her did the rock relent and hold her in its cool embrace. At other times, all it offered her was oppressive heat and stifling humidity. She had never experienced such a sultry climate anywhere before. Ever since the visits from the villagers had stopped, even the air moved like a heavy wall and slapped her on her face. Her mother-in-law's words too bounced on the rock and bombarded her with greater ferocity. Deep down, she knew she could never stay alone in this village ever again. So she had made up her mind to go with him wherever he went.

Virichipalayam was far away. Bicycling over the bumpy roads was not an easy task. She knew he was strong—his body usually felt firm like steel under her fingers. But now she felt bad for him, seeing how far he had to travel to conduct his business. But he did not seem to consider this a difficulty.

He laughed and said, 'Every day, I carry the weight of soda bottles. You are like a light flower compared to them. When I pedal with you sitting behind me, I feel like I am flying!'

His face was drenched in sweat. The fact that he could still keep up a conversation amazed her. Nothing ever seemed to ruffle him. When they encountered a steep incline or large bump in the road, she insisted on making him stop the bicycle so that she could alight and walk alongside. She was also keen that they stop somewhere on the way to eat before resuming their journey. However, he reasoned that it would be difficult for him to ride the bicycle on a full stomach, so it would be better if they ate once they reached the shop.

Barren lands stretched on either side of them. 'Come and see these fields a month from now,' Kumaresan chatted enthusiastically. 'They will be lush green with groundnut crop. Once we get one strong bout of rain, everything will change.'

She sighed. A bout of rain that could change everything?

Saroja liked Virichipalayam immediately. There were a lot of shops along the roads. It felt just like entering a street in Tholur. Small cloth stores, grocery stores, bicycle shops—all arranged in a row. Outside the shops there were some small restaurants where elderly or middle-aged women could be seen sitting with their large idli pots. Saroja looked excitedly at the steam that rose from the piping hot idlis they served. She wanted to eat idlis here one day. Some shops were housed merely in thatched sheds, but they were all crowded. Every shop had a large boiler for tea in the front. They were all clean and marked with holy ash.

'Do you want to drink tea?' he asked her. Even though they would be eating as soon as they reached the shop, she did want some tea first. She looked with wonder at the way they washed the glass tumblers first in regular water and then with hot water. The boy at the tea shop poured the tea back and forth between tumblers until it was frothing at the top. He then added a little bit of the decoction over the froth and handed the glass to her. This is how you make tea, she said to herself. She hadn't had tea since they had come to Kattuppatti. Back home, in Tholur, it was only after she drank her morning cup of tea that she could go about her tasks. But she would not get that here. She hesitated to ask Kumaresan, knowing that her mother-in-law would proba-bly say something hurtful. She had decided she would rather give up drinking tea than brave that.

There was a large open ground on the right side of the road. 'The Saturday fair happens here,' said Kumaresan. She pictured it in her mind—a place filled with shops, crowds of people wandering about, taking in the sights. She imagined herself as one in the crowd, walking among the multitudes. No one there to point to her and ask, 'Who is she? What is her caste?' No one to say, 'She is a witch, she bewitched him.' Nobody in that crowd cared about how many sovereigns of gold she had brought with her. No one who would say, 'We are excommunicating you from the village.' She didn't have to hesitate or be afraid to bargain. She could fight.

Kumaresan kept explaining to her many things about the town, but she didn't really pay much attention. She was still walking through her imaginary crowd, buying bangles at a shop in the fair, happily strolling about on the dusty grounds. It was all very exciting. How lovely to just be one in so many, she thought. Going away from the crowd was the reason for her unhappiness. Could she get back to it now? Would they accept her again? What if she merged with the multitude at the fair? These thoughts swarmed inside her.

By then, they had arrived at the shop Kumaresan had rented. It was only when he stopped balancing with one foot on the ground and said, 'Get down, girl,' did she snap out of her reverie. When they were in Tholur, he used to secretly call her 'pilla'. There it meant 'boy'. But here it meant 'girl'. Initially, she did not understand why he called her that, but she grew to like it. 'Here, that is how men address their wives, pilla,' he laughed. He had a way of unearthing the happiness that was buried in her heart. Beaming, she had thought, may this 'pilla' be the beginning of his untiring efforts to make her belong in this place.

The shop was on a narrow street. It had a low entrance, so they had to bend their heads in order to enter. Inside, there was just one room, but a spacious one. They could lie down and roll around there. Things lay strewn about. The soda machine had not yet arrived.

'I have ordered a trough for the water. I need to go pick it up first,' he said out loud, but mostly to himself.

She realized he was getting into his 'work' frame of mind. 'Eat and then go,' she said.

As they sat down to eat, he told her about the shop. The rent was ten rupees a month. It had a brick-tiled roof. The landlord lived in the next street, and owned four or five such small houses. Listening to him on the way and thinking about the town had made Saroja forget her hunger. Now, when she opened the boxes, it came rushing back, and she ate with great relish. She realized she hadn't eaten like this since she had arrived at Kumaresan's place.

'You make a delicious kozhambu, pilla,' he said.

He too always ate in a fearful hurry when they were at the farmstead, she realized. He had not really enjoyed the food and commented on it. His words of appreciation touched her heart, bringing tears to her eyes. But she didn't let him see her tear up. She bowed her head and finished the food on her plate. It was only after he left to take care of some work outside, and she had seen him off, that she came back into the shop and broke into tears.

She did not know why this town reminded her of Tholur. Even this room reminded her of her home. People of all castes must mingle with each other here, she thought. Even so, there were sure to be people like Mythili akka too. But so what? They wouldn't be able to cause too much trouble. There were probably only ten or fifteen streets in this town, but it felt like a small part of Tholur. She imagined that if she were to live here, one day, while walking these streets, she might suddenly find herself in Tholur.

Why can't we move here? Will Kumaresan agree to this idea? Will he be able to leave his mother? He had stayed apart from his mother for over a year in Tholur, returning home only once in a while to see her. His mother could stay by herself; she didn't even need anyone to talk to. She was happy with her goats. She could talk to them . . . Saroja decided to slowly broach the subject with him. But then she wondered if he would think that this was her way of separating mother and son. Nonetheless, if they indeed left, then perhaps the village would accept Marayi again. Kumaresan could always visit her once in a while secretly in the night.

Besides, what did he know about living with his mother? He left in the mornings and only came back home at night. If he stayed at home, he'd know what it was to live with Marayi. Like constantly walking on fire. Would he be able to understand her? Wiping her tears, she rose. The shop was covered in dust everywhere, and things lay haphazardly. If she sat down to mope about things now, she would be crying until he returned. But if there was a task to be done, then it would distract her from her burdensome thoughts. And as she went about completing the task, the burden would feel lighter and lighter, until, when she finished, there would be no more burden left to bear. Back at the hut on the rock, she was scared to take up any task—after all, she never quite knew what her mother-in-law might say. But here in this shop, in this town, there was no one to stop her.

She swept the entrance clean. The street was not a paved one, just a mud path. She felt strange about sweeping the entrance so long after sunrise, but she told herself it was all right, because this was a shop—not a house. After sweeping, she sprinkled water to make the dust settle down. Then she swept the ground again. As she was engaged in this task, a few people came out of the neighbouring shops and stood watching her. She gave them a friendly smile. They smiled back. True smiles. Happy smiles.

One of the women said, 'Are you going to move here to live?'

In her heart, Saroja blessed the woman for giving words to her wish, and replied, 'We will know soon.'

'When there is a woman to take care of it, any place looks good,' said another woman. 'The boy came here ten days ago saying there would be a shop here soon. But I didn't see him sweeping the entrance. I hope he cleaned the inside at least.' Then she suggested, 'You come now and then and keep the place clean for him.'

It made Saroja happy just to listen to their talk. She had no doubt whatsoever. This was her town. This was her Tholur.

THIRTEEN

Saroja did not feel like leaving Virichipalayam. It took her a long time to thoroughly clean that one room where Kumaresan's shop would soon be housed. It was bigger than the room he had occupied back in Tholur. Once she put things away neatly and managed to sweep the floor and set everything in order, she realized that the room was large enough to accommodate not only the shop but also, possibly, their living quarters. All their belongings and the stove wouldn't take up more than a corner. There were some shelves too—wooden planks mounted on the wall. All this was more than enough for them to make a home right there. The concrete on the floor had eroded in a few places, leaving small pits here and there. But that could be taken care of with a little cement. Saroja continued chatting with the women, her neighbours, as she cleaned.

It was a while before Kumaresan returned, and soon after three empty water tanks arrived in a bullock cart. Moving them into the shop proved to be a rather difficult task. Once they were in, it looked like most of the room had been occupied. Though he told her that he needed to get everything ready in a week so that he could begin delivering soda bottles, it looked like he was only talking to himself. He was very happy that she had cleaned and readied the room. Saroja wondered if she should make use of that moment and ask him right away if they could move to this town. But she did not want to ruin his current state of happiness, so she refrained.

Once they finished eating lunch, he insisted that they leave right away. He wanted to get back home in time to leave for the coming-of-age ceremony at Chellakka's house. Saroja was immediately unsettled. She feared that if she attended the ceremony, some adversity would strike—something that could drain away all the happiness she had gathered today. But she didn't think he would listen to her now. His goal was to make his relatives accept his marriage and receive them as a couple. All his actions were now geared towards that end. His love for her had not wavered even after all that had happened. He believed that his relatives would undergo a magical change of heart and embrace the young couple. But she was sceptical. To her, it didn't look as though his people would ever come around. But he had to realize that himself.

On their way back, they stopped at Kunnoor to buy the things they needed to offer on a tray at the function at Chellakka's house, as was the custom. Fruits, mirror, comb, face powder, fabric for a blouse—they purchased everything. They even bought flowers with which to decorate the edges of the plate. And a small brass mug. All of this cost nearly fifty rupees. When he was trying to save money for the shop, fifty rupees was a considerable expense. But

Chellakka had come in person to invite them, ignoring other people's opinions, and her gesture had made a deep impression on Kumaresan's heart. Otherwise, he was not the kind to spend so much money at once. He said, 'Later, when we hold the function for our daughter, we will get all these back, you see.' She was not sure if he truly believed that or if he was saying it merely to comfort her. Nevertheless, it made her feel strange. Isn't it enough that I am suffering now? Should I give birth to a daughter and watch her suffer too?

When she and Kumaresan were getting married, Periyasami had taken care of all the arrangements before they arrived. He had even taken his sister along to buy new clothes for the newlyweds. They had bought her a sari worth two hundred rupees. Kumaresan had fretted about the expense. 'Why spend so much on a sari you are going to wear only occasionally?' he had said to Saroja. Worried he might also say the same thing to Periyasami, Saroja had warned him: 'They have bought all this with love. Don't say anything to them.' They did not have their own families supporting them, yet here was a stranger doing all he could to help them. True, she would wear that sari only once in a while. But then, they only bought such saris once in a while, didn't they? There was no way she could tell him that then. In his opinion, spending money on anything that was not of daily use was not worth it. Now they were going to a special function celebrating a young girl's coming of age. Also, even though he was not Chellakka's own brother by birth, he was like a maternal uncle to the girl.

Saroja wanted some jasmine flowers to wear in her hair. He asked for the price. When they were told that it was a rupee for one forearm's length of a string of jasmine, Kumaresan hesitated a little. But before he could respond, she said, 'We will buy some.' It made him smile. She smiled back, saying, 'You count every paisa.' Then he bought her some tea and the coconut biscuits she was fond of.

Roaming around the streets of Senkundroor and buying things at the shops made her very happy. She could not help thinking how wonderful it would be if things continued in this vein hereon. By the time they returned home, the day had ended and an ashen darkness had started to spread everywhere. Her mother-in-law too had arrived just then and was tethering the goats.

'The entire village is laughing at us, and you want to go about, parading yourselves!' she said spitefully, and punched a goat in its jaw. The animal bleated in pain. Saroja instinctively touched her own cheek. The day had been a happy one until then. How was the rest of it going to be? Her stomach felt as though it was churning. For a few days now, she had been experiencing dizzy spells now and then, but she was not sure why.

It didn't look like Kumaresan paid any attention to what his mother was saying. 'Are you planning to go to the function at Chellakka's house?' he asked.

'I am going all right!' she replied. 'To the cremation ground.'

He simply said, 'Okay, we are going.'

'Sure! Go!' his mother shot back without looking at him. 'Go together as a couple. That's the best way to ensure all the other villages can laugh at us too.'

Kumaresan asked Saroja to get ready. He looked as though his mind was elsewhere, contemplating some deep thought. He is used to his mother's anger, so he must be bothered about something else, Saroja concluded.

'Which fort are you planning to capture now?' she said to him, trying to tease him about looking so preoccupied.

She understood his dilemma only after he explained it to her. Apparently, Chellakka's brothers lived in this village. They would definitely depart from here, with a band of musicians, carrying gift plates for her—seven plates that went from the girl's maternal uncle's house. Others would inevitably join them, regardless of whether they were taking gift plates or not. As the crowd grew, the group would turn into a long procession. In addition to the drumbeat of the melam and resonant notes of the nadaswaram, there would even be revellers doing a folk dance. There was no way Saroja and Kumaresan could be a part of this crowd. Now that the village had issued its decree, they would not be allowed to join the procession. Kumaresan wondered what they could do.

It was too late for her to ask if they really had to go. After all, they had spent quite a bit of money and already bought everything. Rather than bother him, she thought it best to let him mull over it and come to a decision. So she didn't say anything and busied herself with getting ready. She put on the same sari she had for their wedding, and combed her hair and wore the flowers in a long string.

He asked her to take the wide plate covering the large vessel and clean it with some tamarind, but she hesitated as she was not very accustomed to brass vessels. Since he couldn't ask his mother to do it—after all, it might provoke her to say something harsh—he did it himself. Once cleaned, the brass plate shone as bright as the new mug they had purchased that day. Then he helped her arrange everything on it. He kept the two bunches of poovan bananas on two sides of the plate and placed the coconut near one of them. All the other objects went in the middle. Once she spread out the paper flowers and pinned them to the fruits, the plate looked beautiful. She had never seen such a gift plate before. These traditions were new for her.

There was some food leftover from the morning. He said, 'There will be a feast after the function, but it probably won't begin before midnight. You won't be able to go without food for so long; so let's eat a little bit before we leave.'

Since Saroja had arrived in the village, they had been cooking rice. But his mother wouldn't even touch it. She prepared her own food. Whether it was kambu millets or pap, she made it for herself in the cowshed and ate it right there. No one knew when exactly she did the cooking.

Kumaresan tried reasoning with his mother several times: 'Please eat the rice we are making. Why are you lighting a separate fire?'

She had the same curt response each time: 'I placed my trust in you all these years. And you have clearly dishonoured it. From now on, I am alone. I don't expect you to feed me. I have not fallen so low in the world that I would shamelessly eat the food made by just any woman. All I need are a few things. It is enough if you leave me alone and don't touch my belongings.'

Marayi did not change her stance no matter how many times he tried to convince her to eat with them. For the first few days, her words hurt him. But slowly he grew accustomed to her stubbornness. She always found something snide to say about their food: 'They think they can eat rice every day, as though they have a field brimming with harvest here.' Or, 'If the horse is hungry enough, it will eat the oats as well as the grass.'

Now, as they ate the little bit of leftover rice, they could hear the sounds of melam and music.

'The procession from the uncle's house has started,' he said. 'Let's not join them. We'll go by cycle and wait near the temple in Molappalayam. That's where people carrying gift plates from the other villages will gather. We can walk with them.'

She liked his plan; she had feared that he might ask her to go and stand with the village folk here. Even if one person said something, within minutes the entire village would become involved, escalating the matter into a public spectacle. From their hut, they could hear the sound of the distant drums intermittently. Perhaps this was for the kuravan-kurathi folk dance. It was as if the music stopped long enough for them to have a conversation and then resumed.

Saroja and Kumaresan started walking, pushing the bicycle with the plate resting on the rear carrier. They could hear Marayi murmuring to herself again as she lay on the cot on the rock. Saroja often wondered if her mother-in-law would go beyond murmuring and ranting. But Kumaresan had laughingly told her, 'Barking dogs seldom bite.' She reminded herself of that now. But if someone stepped on the tail of a barking dog, wouldn't it bite, she wondered? She shook her head to chase away these thoughts as they progressed on their journey. In the sky to the west, she spotted the moon, just a few feet from the ground, at level with her eyes. He kept talking to her all the way. She realized that he was talking incessantly to distract her from the looming darkness that she had not yet grown used to—a darkness that seemed to engulf them despite the moonlight.

Kumaresan explained that Chellakka had five daughters. She kept bearing children hoping for a boy, but that never happened. Usually, it was for the eldest daughter that maternal uncles went bearing plates of gifts, accompanied by music and drums, but her second and third daughters had attained puberty even before the first one had—a fact that worried Chellakka no end. It was only when the girl came of age at sixteen that Chellakka was relieved. Their plan was to first conduct the ceremony for the eldest daughter and follow it, on the same night, with ceremonies for the other two daughters who had attained puberty earlier. By now they had come quite close to the Pillayar temple in Molappalayam. And, lost in her enjoyment of the narration,

Saroja no longer felt uncomfortable walking in the moonlit night.

They could see a flame torch and two Petromax lamps in front of the Pillayar temple. They could also hear the joyful voices of the people gathered there. One rose loud and clear: 'It looks like it will be morning by the time people from the girls' uncle's family reach here. By then, they'll probably just feed us leftover food.'

Recognizing that voice, Kumaresan said to her, 'That is my eldest uncle.'

Saroja was startled. When she and Kumaresan had visited his grandparents' village, none of his uncles had been present. Now all four of them might be here. She could not imagine what would happen if they all decided to gang up against Kumaresan and herself. Whenever she thought of that trip to his grandparents' home, she found herself feeling intensely relieved that the uncles had not been present.

She had not considered the possibility that Kumaresan's uncles and their families would be part of the crowd here. It had not occurred to her that if Chellakka was related to Kumaresan, she was definitely related to his uncles too. Here, in these parts, everyone within the same caste was related to one another. Kumaresan had a particular way of addressing each one of them. If they were not 'maaman'—uncle—or 'machinan'—brother-in-law—there were other terms like 'pangali' that denoted degrees of distance in kinship.

Why did Saroja not think of this! She shrank and withdrew into herself and hid behind Kumaresan. As they approached the lights, someone said, 'Ada! It is our son-in-law, Nōndi. The procession started from your village. Why didn't you join them?'

Kumaresan replied jokingly, 'I thought that my uncles here might be too deaf to hear the sound of the drums and music, so I felt I should come ahead of the procession and inform you all!'

His eldest uncle stepped forward from the crowd and shouted, 'Whom are you calling deaf? I have watched you grow up. Are you making fun of your elders?'

It was clear that his uncle was in the mood for a fight. 'I didn't say that about you, maama,' he said humbly.

'Don't call me maama. Don't even try to address me as a relative now,' his uncle replied.

Kumaresan did not say anything further. Whatever he said would lead to an argument. It was clear that was what everyone was waiting for. But his uncle didn't stay quiet. 'She looks like she would trip over a blade of grass. He has come here dragging this orphaned dog. Who invited him? At the mere mention of food, all these dogs turn up with their tongues hanging about.'

Saroja did not lift her head to look at anyone, but the words battered her like rocks. Kumaresan had not expected any of this. Shocked, he stayed silent.

Someone else said, 'Why are you fighting here? This is a problem between you two. Take it elsewhere.'

His uncle's wife shouted, 'Their village has ostracized them. Yet here they are, strolling about as a couple! If he truly understood what he has done by marrying someone from who knows where, would he stand so shamelessly in front of the community and speak like this? Would he dare talk back to his uncle, who carried and raised him?'

His uncle followed, thundering, 'Of course he would! He is still enchanted by this new girl and his new job. Once it all sours, he will come back to us, begging.'

As the assembled guests drew near, their numbers swelled into a crowd.

Chellakka, who had come there to welcome her brother's family properly, intervened. 'Please don't fight,' she begged them. 'You are all my relatives who have come for a function at my home. I need both of you. Please don't argue. You can sort it out after the function is over. You will be blessed. Please.'

But Kumaresan's eldest uncle spoke loudly and decisively to his wife, 'Pilla, let's leave. Call our children. What business can I have at any place where he is going to be present?'

FOURTEEN

Saroja didn't rise from the cot for most of the following day.

In the morning, Kumaresan woke her up, saying, 'Shall we go, pilla?'

Since he knew she had been terrified after the altercation with his uncle in Molappalayam, he wanted to take her with him to the shop now. She too wanted to go with him but as soon as she got up, she felt faint. She found that she couldn't even sit up properly, and sank back down.

'You go and come back soon,' she whimpered.

'Get up, make some food and eat,' he coaxed. 'Otherwise, the child will be hungry.'

She didn't understand him at first. Opening her eyes with great difficulty, she looked at him. In the dark hut, his smile shone brilliantly.

'What are you saying?' she said.

He sat next to her and softly touched her head. Brushing aside the stray strands of hair on her forehead, he gently kissed her there. In that moment, his face bore no trace of regret about the way things had transpired the day before. He seemed to be filled with a great joy.

'I can tell from the way you feel faint,' he said tenderly. 'That's what it is. How often have I heard it! We can't tell amma now. It will just upset her more. We'll tell her later, gently. You have to take care of yourself.'

'I lie huddled here because I am petrified thinking of all your fights. And here you are, with this other idea! Are you teasing me?'

'No, no, pilla. I can tell by looking at your face. A new life has entered you.'

Infected by his enthusiasm, she shyly closed her eyes. His breath brushed against her cheek and he kissed her softly. She did not know when he left. She lay there, basking in the afterglow of his kisses. She could not sleep; nor could she stay awake. A flurry of images ran across her mind, but she could not see any of them clearly.

She dreamed that she had asked, 'Is it a boy or a girl?' to which he replied, 'Both.' Then she whispered to herself, 'Don't be greedy!' She saw her father and brother too—her father holding her hand and telling her something. Kumaresan's uncles appeared with their angry faces, and vanished. A herd of goats was running towards her. Once they drew near, all of them turned into her mother-in-law. She saw children running and playing on the rock. And Kumaresan was running after them, yelling, 'Careful, careful!' Vellapayyan came to her and said, 'Were they all born to Kumaresan?' The old woman, the vegetable vendor, said, 'You have saved yourself this way. If you hadn't given birth to them, they'd have killed you long ago.' Then Velayi appeared and said, 'Will you tie the sari on me with the pleats in front?'

Someone said furiously, 'The rules apply to the child too!' Then she saw many other people she didn't know, whose faces she couldn't see clearly. As she lay there, confused and dazed, her famished stomach woke her up.

When she staggered outside the hut, the sun assaulted her face. She lowered her eyes, trying to adjust to the burning glare. The fear that she might fall down if she tried to walk further gripped her. Only after she splashed some cold water on her face did she regain some sense of clarity. She could see the wide expanse of the fields and the palm trees, and hear the cawing of crows. But there was not a single person in sight. No one came to the rock these days. Earlier, even if the visitors only said rude things, at least the sight of their faces provided some relief from the punishing monotony of life here. But not any more. It had been days since she had even heard the footsteps of passers-by.

She recalled her mother-in-law's rant from her dream: 'Her arrival has made sure nobody visits us any longer. Who knows what else she is going to deprive us of?' Or was it not part of the dream? Had Marayi actually said that while Saroja lay faint on the cot inside?

At night, she could hear the sound of the melam drums from the temple, marking the beginning of the festival. She did not know when they would make the pongal offering. What would she do even if she did know? What would the village decide after the festival? It would be better if they moved to Virichipalayam before that. Given the tenderness and concern with which Kumaresan had woken her that morning, she was hopeful that he might now agree to the idea of moving to Virichipalayam. If she really was pregnant, he wouldn't leave her here. In Virichipalayam, there were all those women in the neighbouring houses—they would help her. They were just like her neighbours back in Tholur. If she insisted with him now, she was sure he'd agree to move. As she sat down on the rock, her stomach cramped and tightened. She had not eaten properly the night before. Since they had expected to eat at the feast at Chellakka's house, they had not prepared any food at home. However, they had to return from the ceremony without having anything. They had no desire for food at the time, so they went to bed after eating what little was left in the pot at home. She was hungry now, but there was nothing in the pot. Her mother-in-law must have cooked some food for herself. If she ate a little of that, Marayi wouldn't find out, would she? She looked around her, but she could not spot her mother-in-law anywhere in the vicinity. She must have gone quite a distance, herding the goats.

Saroja got up and walked into the hut in front of her. Until then, she had not even peeped inside. The hut had no solid walls, just thatched palm fronds all around, held together to form an enclosure. There were baskets and spades lying scattered in front of the hut. Inside, in a corner, she spotted the vessels in which her mother-in-law cooked her food. They were all mud pots. She removed the lid of the rice pot that had been kept on the stove. Immediately, the scent of cooked kambu millets pierced her nose. She could even make out the dip in the rice where a ladleful had been scooped out.

She walked back into her hut and fetched a plate and a ladle. Using the ladle in such a way that it wouldn't leave an obvious dip in the pot of rice, she took out half a ladleful. When she looked into the pot, she was satisfied that her mother-in-law wouldn't know that some of the kambu had been taken. It looked like there was some kozhambu in the pot next to the stove, but it turned out to be some powder. She threw some on top of the kambu on her plate and rushed out. Sitting inside her hut, she wolfed down the meal, barely pausing to chew and swallow. The kambu millets and the powder together were very spicy. Eating just a little bit brought on a bout of hiccups, so she drank some water.

Once her hunger subsided and she could think more clearly, she felt like crying. This was stolen food. She had to steal food in her own house. She lamented her fate, that there was no one to rush to her side, knowing her condition, and take care of her lovingly. If her mother-in-law had seen her taking the food, she might have called her a thief and chased her away. She tried pushing these thoughts away and turned her attention to finishing the food on the plate. The powder had been made from groundnut; it went great with kambu millets. Would Marayi realize that some food had been taken from her pot? Saroja had been careful not to make it obvious. For a brief moment, she felt absurdly pleased about being a good thief.

As a child, she used to steal money from her father's and brother's shirt pockets and buy the sweets she liked as well as candies for her playmates. She had gone to school until the fifth standard, and recalled always having a bunch of children following her. It was her brother who discovered her thieving; he had slapped her. 'Please don't hit the child,' her father had told her brother. To her he had merely said, 'My dear, if you need money, just ask me.' She had cried then. After that episode, her father asked her every day, 'How much money do you want?' Her brother never asked; he just gave her some change. Clearly, the thieving she had practised then was coming to her aid now.

Energized by the meal, she cooked some food, making enough for the night as well, and ate some more. Suddenly, she began to feel very tired. She shut the door to the hut, lay on the cot and slept for hours. Again, it was hunger that roused her. She ate again without any sense of what time of the day it was, and came out and sat on the rock. She could hear her mother-in-law returning in the distance, herding the goats back home. She was thankful for the animals, for they bore the brunt of her mother-in-law's anger. Her gaze shifted towards the path by which Kumaresan would come home, and then moved away. She did not know when he would return. If he worked hard for the next four or five days, he could open the shop soon.

She had not expected such a row to erupt during the function at Chellakka's house. Kumaresan's eldest uncle was furious. For a moment it had seemed like he meant to hit Kumaresan. But Kumaresan had stood his ground silently, troubled and teary-eyed. He knew that it was best to remain silent. If people could find fault with him even when he wasn't saying anything, she could imagine what would have happened if he had. No one came to his support. They all just demanded, 'Why are you fighting here?'

'Why did Chella invite them when their own village has rejected them? What's the need for him to come and fulfil his duties as a distant uncle to the girls?'

'Chella's daughter has finally come of age after all these years. Don't interrupt the function here with your personal argument.'

'Hey, Nōndi, don't you see how infuriated your uncle is? Why are you still here? Go away. Is it proper to create trouble at an auspicious event?'

All this commotion had started even before the girls' maternal uncle and family arrived at the head of their procession. It occurred to Saroja that things would only escalate once that other crowd arrived. She pressed Kumaresan's hand, trying to communicate that it would be best if they returned home. In all the cacophony, she could not hear anything clearly. Suddenly, his uncle rushed forward like a charging bull, casting away all restraint, and kicked the plate Kumaresan held in his hand. In the darkness, they could only hear the brass plate and mug flying and landing somewhere out of sight.

'You wretched dog who feasts on waste!' his uncle hollered. 'Taking pity on you because you were a fatherless child, we carried you on our shoulders, we raised you. And *this* is how you show your gratitude to us! The moment you see a little money, you forget all that we have done for you? You call this a marriage? I will break your head open! Go away! Go die, like your father did. We have cared for our widowed sister so far. We will keep doing that even if you are gone.'

Kumaresan stood motionless. Somebody dragged his uncle away. A few people also tried to nudge Kumaresan, to send him on his way. In the meantime, someone had gathered the plate and the things that lay scattered, and handed all of them back to Saroja.

As they walked back home, pushing the bicycle along, the clamour of the festivities followed them for a long time. Kumaresan and Saroja did not say anything to each other. In the oppressive silence, they could hear each other breathing. When they reached the rock, Kumaresan broke down.

His mother, who was lying on a cot on the rock, chastised him. 'You should have expected this! What were you thinking?'

His whimpers ceased immediately. The rock and the fields lay spread out in all directions, but there was no spot where he could go and cry out his grief. He could not expect any support now from the mother who had raised him lovingly all these years. She did not have one kind word to say to him; instead her tirade continued unabated. Her words tore into him like a dog ripping away flesh from bone. He kept quiet and did not respond while her angry comments became louder and more vigorous.

Have I done such a terrible thing, he wondered. Was it such a sin to get married? Can't I marry the woman I love? In what way have I wronged anyone by doing that? She loves me with all her life. I love her the same way. I have not gone to anyone asking for money. Why is everyone driving us away? Even amma refuses to understand this. I will be a good husband no matter whom I marry. What's the harm in marrying the woman I love? And why should they point out that they carried me on their shoulders, that they raised me? Isn't that how everyone brings up their children? I am not denying they did that for me, am I? At my uncle's house, they keep saying that they did this and they did that . . . What exactly did they do? They were merely protecting their own. Did they build us a tile-roofed house here on the rock? Did they spend their own money on us? Caste! Which caste is Soda Shop Bhai from? Wasn't he the one who offered me the job? If he hadn't done that, how could I have made some money? No man from my caste came to my aid.

Kumaresan wanted to ask his mother all this. But thinking of her life as a young widow who had lived alone on this farmstead all these years and raised him all by herself, he didn't say anything for a while out of respect. But when he was unable to restrain himself any more, he finally said, 'Amma, you keep pointing out everything you've done for me, but if you really loved me, would you stand in the way of my happiness? Let the people from the village say whatever they want to say. Who cares about the uncles and the other fools? You tell me, did you raise me with love? You only took care of me because you needed some sort of stability in life. You don't really love me at all. If you did, you wouldn't be spewing fire at me the way you have been doing every day for so long. Look at her. If you had given birth to a daughter, she'd look just like her. You are a woman too. Please don't talk about love. It's all such humbug.'

His mother wasn't one to stay quiet. This was the first time they were talking it out. 'That's right!' she shrieked. 'The village is more important to me than you. Do you think you can survive, without anyone's support? I have been living alone, without associating with any man, since I was twenty years old, haven't I? How can you be so weak for the body's pleasures at *this* age?'

'If I can't have desires at twenty, then when am I supposed to have them? When I am sixty? Amma, just because you suffered in life, does that mean I should too? If you had belonged to some other caste where widows can remarry, they might have got you married again. You'd have experienced life's difficulties differently. Having lived alone all your life, what do you know?'

'Fine!' she spat. 'I know *nothing*. You know everything. *She* has taught you everything! Otherwise, would you dare talk back to me like this? Is this how I raised you? The moment you laid eyes on her, your own mother became an outsider to you. I shouldn't have let things go this far. Do you think you can live happily after incurring my wrath? A mother's curse will follow you to other lifetimes too!'

Saroja stopped him from responding to this outburst. She did not have the strength to witness another screaming match. But his mother continued to rant and rave. Even when Saroja woke up in the middle of the night, she could hear her mother-in-law's laments. She wallowed in her misery, singing all night long. She didn't sleep all night. Kumaresan too must have heard her. How did she manage to come up with these songs?

But that was two days ago. The following day, before he left the farmstead, Kumaresan told Saroja that he would either return late or spend the night in town and return the next evening. He kept telling her his plans: that he intended to clean the bottles and start filling them with soda in the night; that he had sent for Periyasami to come and help him; that he would return latest by evening the next day; that he planned to go to the Saturday market to sell cool drinks. She neither heard nor understood him fully.

The thought that the shop would be ready soon brought her immense relief. They could move soon to Virichipalayam. But she was not sure she could spend two days here without him nearby. The giddiness that started in the morning began to settle down only by the afternoon. At night, she could not fall asleep easily even when he was with her. With him away, it would be even worse. She would lie there, expecting to hear the familiar sound of his bicycle.

'Doesn't matter how late it is,' she had pleaded. 'Please come back home. I can't be here alone.'

Though she felt better that day, she still could not walk without fearing that she might fall down. She felt guilty about not being able to cook and send food with Kumaresan for the past two days. But given her condition, she just couldn't get up and cook. There were a lot of restaurants in Virichipalayam; he could always eat in one of those. But she had to cook for herself. She was lucky that her mother-in-law had not found out that Saroja had stolen her food. But she couldn't expect to do that every day.

At midday, Saroja woke up and completed her tasks one by one. After she was done with them all, she fell in a heap on the cot, barely conscious of her surroundings. It was only once she ate lunch that she acquired some sense of clarity, which got even better towards the evening, when she had no other work besides awaiting Kumaresan's return. All she had for company were the birds flying back to their nests. She had discovered so many birds since coming here. Do they have worries like humans do, she wondered. Were there birds that waited for their husbands just like she was doing?

Only a few birds sought refuge in the palm tree. Along the path that led away from the rock and meandered along a brook were large trees and dense bushes. A variety of bird sounds could be heard from there well past dusk. That evening, she was so immersed in the symphony of chirping and twittering that she did not realize how much time had passed before the noises ceased. Her stomach rumbled again; she needed to relieve herself. All her schedules had gone awry since her arrival on the rock. She was accustomed to using proper bathrooms in Tholur, so her stomach refused to empty itself when she sat in the outdoors. Now that her bowels no longer followed a fixed routine, her stomach started urging her whenever it felt like emptying itself.

When she got up, she realized that darkness had gathered everywhere. A while back, she had found herself a spot within the bushes in the nearby ditch—a place that gave her a little privacy. She quickly walked towards that spot now. This was the first time she had come here in the dark. The buzz of the insects swarming about pierced her ears. She parted the darkness with her hands as she walked into the bush and sat down there. In her fear, her stomach refused to oblige.

As she got up and tried to walk away without soiling her feet, she heard whispers—snatches of human conversation amidst the piercing buzz of insects. She stood, frozen in fear, and tried to listen closely. That was when she discerned her mother-in-law's voice. Even when Marayi murmured to herself, it sounded like she was arguing with an opponent.

'I am patient only for one reason,' Marayi was saying. 'I don't want any harm to come to him. He has started talking back to me now! He used to be such an obedient boy; she has changed him. I have controlled myself all these days only for his sake. Otherwise, I'd have cut her throat with the sharp edge of the palm frond and ended it all long ago.'

The sound of another voice startled Saroja. 'We'll take care of it. Don't worry!' it said. 'He will come to no harm. We can make sure it is all done within an hour. The village headman is our man. He will take care of it. When the entire village is on our side, what's there to fear?'

Try as she might, she could not recognize that male voice. No matter how much she thought about it, she just could not place it.

FIFTEEN

Saroja could not tell which direction the sounds were coming from. But she instinctively cautioned herself against revealing her presence in any way. She was rooted to the spot, like a dark statue in the bushes, as she tried to listen to every word. Marayi spoke loudly, while the other voice reached her in fragmented whispers. Therefore, she had to make sense of the conversation based on what her mother-in-law was saying.

'Where did you find Bhai Anna?' asked Marayi.

The man responded, 'Bhai Anna hasn't been here since Nōndi returned with this girl. It looked like he had decided to go to different villages. But we waited patiently. After all, he had to come here at some point, didn't he?'

'Bhai Anna is a good man. He only wanted to help us. How could he have known where our dog went about lifting his leg?'

'It wouldn't have mattered if he had found a girl from one of our castes. Now this has become such a dishonourable affair.'

'Was it true what Bhai Anna said?'

'We took him with us straight to Tholur and made our own inquiries. Her father and brother work in a leather factory. They live in a one-room house that is as small as a sparrow's nest. Because it is the town, the people who live nearby belong to different castes.'

'Do they all talk and mix with each other?'

'They might talk to each other, but do you think they will actually mix? No.'

'What did you ask them?'

'We just said that we were looking for the boy who went there to work. The family doesn't know that they've come here. They thought the two had run away. So we told them that they haven't come here. Apparently, the father and son said, "Let her get lost, we can't be looking for her." They must have known about the boy, and decided to keep quiet because they know our boy is from a good family.'

'We won't face any trouble from there, will we?'

'Nothing. Bhai Anna won't come here again. Who is going to give them the news, then? If they hear of it from somewhere and come here, we can fake some tears and say we didn't think she would do that to herself. No one has to teach you to raise a dirge! What can they do after that? They have no one here.'

Suddenly Saroja heard four or five more voices, and the distinct sounds of more people approaching over the pathway. She began to tremble in fear. Their plans seemed clear and decisive at one instant and then muddled and confused the next. They had gone to Tholur to find out about her! She had thought that all they would do was cast them out of the village and cut off all communication with them. They had clearly gone way beyond that.

Her mother-in-law had never said a kind word to her. Saroja also realized that she did not know where exactly Marayi went, or whom she met, when she went herding the goats during the day. Kumaresan did not think his mother was capable of inflicting any harm, but now Saroja's body shivered in fear. She could not think clearly. The conspirators were whispering to one another now. Since the wind changed direction, she could not hear them clearly any longer. But what more did she need to hear?

She sat back down in that dark bush. The thorny plants that made up that bush closed around her and protected her. A short outgrowth of neem from within the thicket had spread its branches like an umbrella. Through its canopy, she could spot a few stars. Initially, she had been terrified to come here on her own even during the day. She would ask Kumaresan to accompany her and make him wait some distance away while she did her business. It had taken her some time to get used to coming here alone. Of late, there were moments when she felt safer among these wild bushes than trapped inside the hut on the rock. Before long, this spot had become a refuge where she could shed some tears in privacy and separate herself from all the things going on in her life. Kumaresan had told her several times that there were a lot of insects and bugs here. He even showed her an alternative spot out in the fields. But she had rejected it because she suspected that people could see her from the outside. This was the best spot.

So far, she had not seen any snakes. Rats ran by sometimes. Once, she saw a rabbit. It ran away in fear as soon as it noticed her. She didn't know where this long stretch of bushes ended, but within its giant, outstretched arms she had found a haven. She had started to enjoy spending time here, sitting inside this private bower of sorts.

Kumaresan even made fun of her: 'In Tholur, no one knew when you went into the toilet and when you stepped out. Here, once you go into the bush, it takes you an hour to get out!' She didn't know how else to respond to that but with a laugh. She had often thought that thorns and bushes were far better than human beings. And here she was proven correct. She sat huddled there, like a baby bird waiting for her mother to return with food.

He stomach tightened, and she started crying despite herself. Utter darkness surrounded her, and her eyes did not have the power to pierce through it. But her ears were sharper than ever before. She discerned even the faintest rustle of leaves with utmost clarity. The voices that she had heard closer to the bush a little while ago now seemed to come from near the rock. From there, they sounded like the meaningless chatter of the crows.

She expected to hear Kumaresan's bicycle along the path close to the bush where she was hiding. She would recognize that sound anywhere. After every two turns of the wheel the bicycle emitted a screech. And the whirr of the rotating chain was very much like the buzz of insects. She could tell those sounds apart even in her sleep. Everything would be all right if she heard them now. Everything would change for the better. But it was only the noises from the rock that grew louder. Suddenly she heard people walking near the bush.

One of them squatted, spat on the ground, and said, 'Where could she have gone?'

'Didn't that akka say that she saw her when she was tying the goats? How far could she have gone then?'

'She must have run into the fields? She couldn't have gone too far.'

'But two people have gone to look near the bus stop, just in case. There are no buses at this time. We will find her.'

'Maybe she is destined to live long.'

The voices receded and went towards the rock. She realized that a crowd had assembled at the rock. Of all days, Kumaresan had told her today that he might not return home tonight. Her mother-in-law must have heard him, and made these arrangements. Or perhaps those men had just returned after finding out information from this person they called Bhai Anna.

She did not know what they planned to do to her. Would they club her down? Or would she be hacked to death with sickles? Was she destined to live long, as one of the voices had complained? People lived around here in all directions. There was nowhere she could seek help. At least they wouldn't look for her here for a while. Until the night ended, she had to stay hunched here somehow. She would be safe once Kumaresan returned. He would not let anyone harm her. He was her only refuge.

In her heart, she prayed to her favourite goddess, Kali. Once, Kumaresan took her to the temple that was a mile from here. With widened eyes, her tongue sticking out, and a glowing face, Kali had appeared fearsome. Saroja took an immediate liking to the goddess. She had felt that this female deity had the power to destroy everything.

She heard some voices close to the bush again.

'We can start the prayers at the temple only after everything gets done here. That's why we asked people to wait for a while. But it looks like this won't happen today. She must have suspected something and run away.'

'Someone should have watched her movements from the evening onwards. We have lost her now.'

'She must be here somewhere. She might even be hiding inside this bush.'

When she heard that, her heart stopped. Goddess Kali was not going to help her. She was, after all, *their* goddess. She realized that it was towards her that Kali's wrath was directed. That must have been why the goddess betrayed her hideout as soon as Saroja prayed to her. But in her panic, she had not been able to think of any other god quickly enough. In Tholur, she went to the temple only once in a while. Then, she hadn't known what exactly to pray for; she had everything she wanted. She would just say in her heart, 'May everyone be well.'

After she started falling in love with Kumaresan, her prayers had become more specific. 'I want him.' Once, after they visited the Kōttaicchaami temple in Tholur together, he asked her, 'What did you pray for?' She said, 'I asked for you.' He laughed, 'Really?' Teasing her, he had said, 'If we ask for such things from god, we need to give something in return. What are you going to give?' She felt bad for not promising a return gift. Seeing her muttering to herself, he said, 'What are you doing?' At the time, she did not give him a proper response, just smiled at him. Later, he had asked her about it again. Finally she had admitted, 'I prayed, "Please give him to me. I am ready even to give away my life."' He said, 'Then what will happen to me? That's not how you pray! You can promise to offer a goat or some pongal.'

Kōttaicchaami was a powerful god. He would definitely expect fulfilment of promises made to him. Had he sent these people? Was he saying, 'I answered your prayers. Now give me your life.' Terrified, confused, and filled with these thoughts, she could not hear the voices any more. Would they look for her in the bush after they had searched everywhere else? Her mother-in-law knew that she used this bush as her toilet. She might remember that and send the men to hunt for her in here.

She did not know how many they were and what weapons they carried. Now the voices from the rock came loud and clear. The entire village must have made a collective decision about this. She heard voices near the bush again.

'Our Vellapayyan can finish everything in two minutes. All we need to do is to find her.'

'There's a crowd now. If I had found her earlier, I'd thought I would enjoy the fair-skinned girl that has bewitched Nōndi. Now it is too late.'

'We can still enjoy her once we've caught her.'

Saroja was sweating profusely. The hideout within the thicket was not going to protect her for too long. She contemplated slowly inching further into the bush, as far as she could. The thorns would tear her skin, and there might even be snakes, but so what? Suddenly, she started thinking clearly. Holding her arms tight across her chest, she tried to move her feet slowly, but they refused to budge. With great effort, she tried again, and felt like she had managed to move ahead just a bit. She told herself that if she moved to the left, she'd be moving further into the bush. It did not matter if she died of snakebite or because she was stung by an insect. She could not let these people catch her. Surely her destiny had not brought her all the way here to succumb to these ruffians.

Her body suddenly slammed against an obstacle. A tree.

Immediately, she heard someone cry out, 'Hey, look, there! The tree inside the bush is moving!'

The sound of someone coming running.

Seized by great terror, her entire body drenched in sweat and tears, she crawled on all fours like a centipede scrambling to avoid being trampled underfoot, and started moving slowly and purposefully, determined to escape.

SIXTEEN

With every move Saroja made, some of the plants in the bush shuddered and swayed.

Would even the plants and trees betray her now?

I have come placing my trust in you. How can you betray me like this? She pleaded with every little thing her hands touched. She imagined the roots and stems of the plants to be human feet and clasped them tightly, touching them, begging them for mercy.

But they paid her no heed. Like fluttering flags that could arrest one's attention even from a distance, everything she touched nodded and shook its head, signaling her presence. The insects that had been sitting in these plants now rose up and swarmed above in a buzzing cloud, their drone travelling through the air. The birds that had built their nests in the bush were confused at this intrusion and they flew about, not knowing where to perch. She too did not know what she was doing or where she could go.

As her anxiety about being spotted mounted, she ended up rustling and shaking everything. The voices now seemed certain that she was inside the bush. They shouted in excitement, 'Dey! Come here. She is here.' The sound of people rushing towards the bush assailed her. She shut her ears tight with her hands, but she could not stop the noise. It fell upon her ears like a large hammer pounding on a rock.

Voices and footsteps blended with one another. Though she could not hear clearly what people were saying, she knew what their intentions were. What she didn't know was how far into the bush she had managed to move. It felt like she could keep going. But the voices seemed to be getting closer. She would feel better if she managed to get to a place from where she couldn't hear them. Suddenly, she realized that they were haphazardly hitting at the bush with their sticks. Every time the sticks fell on the plants, it felt like they were falling on her back. The plants that were already withered in the heat showed no resistance to these beatings.

'How deep could she have gone? Come on, let's find out. If a woman—no, a girl—can be so bold, then what's the use of us being men?'

'There are a lot of snakes inside this bush. It was only yesterday that I saw one. Who knows what she might get bitten by?

'Look at her trying to fool us! We should have done this as soon as she set foot in the village. It is our fault that we left her alive for so long.'

A root that Saroja had clutched started twisting around her wrist. A snake! She shook her hand desperately to rid herself of it. But it did not release her. She felt as though it was coiling itself around her arm, wringing it. Then, as she twisted and turned, it seemed to slither towards her shoulder and tighten itself around her neck. Her entire body was now caught in its terrible hold. She tried to get up and run, but it was impossible. Even if she tried raising her head a little bit, she risked getting mauled by a tangle of branches and thorns that hovered menacingly above her. Then, suddenly, the snake was gone. Was it even a snake? Or was it just a creeper that had wound itself around her while she struggled desperately in the thicket?

Not pausing to ruminate, she shuffled along, staying low. She decided that she would not stay still, no matter what. She moved into every little gap and crevice she could find between the trees and plants. Yet, the voices advanced on her. In her heart, she pleaded, 'I have not harmed any of you. Why do you torment me like this?'

As if they heard her prayer, the voices ceased, as did the sound of sticks beating down on the bushes.

She wanted to make use of this moment and plunge further into the bush. Thorns tore at her palm. Until she'd found this bush, she had suffered immensely. In the mornings or during the day, she could not go out into the fields to relieve herself. She'd wait for it to get dark and then she would ask Kumaresan to take her and wait at a distance. Even then, despite the engulfing darkness, she felt exposed, as though she was sitting inside an open room. Also, with someone standing not far away, how could she relieve herself?

One morning, when Kumaresan was away, her stomach churned and she had found this bush. At first, she had been scared to enter it, but soon she realized there was a safe spot inside. From then on, she had made this her spot. But each time she went there, Kumaresan warned her.

'It is full of karuvela thorns. Even if they scratch you, they'll cause great pain. If a thorn pierces your flesh, it is poisonous. We are all used to this place. We know where to place our feet. We will sit down, safely out of the way of the thorns; but you don't know enough to do all that. So please don't go too far into the bush. Don't worry, no one comes here.'

If he was at home, he'd wait for her near the rock until she was done relieving herself in the bush. On most days, she used the spot only when he was at home. Now his warnings returned to haunt her. You told me not to go further into the bush, but today you have left me to fend for myself. Why don't you come back? Couldn't you have forced me to go to Virichipalayam with you? You've left me, cast me into a poisonous nest. Kumaresa! Can you hear me? Where is the sound of your bicycle?

Once again, she heard voices right outside the bush. Flashlights started tearing into the darkness. She heard more voices now parting the bush. Had they been waiting patiently for just this moment all these days? All that kindness she had heard in some of the voices—was all of that false? Were none of these people true?

'If I get hold of her, I will catch her by her hair and thrash her. Look at how much trouble she is causing us!'

'Looks like she's not blessed with a painless death. She seems destined to die by getting torn about by the thorns here.'

'She must be sitting huddled somewhere like a wet chicken. She could not have gone too far.'

They could not brave the thorns beyond a point. Nor could the light from their torches reach where she was. If she stayed here all night, they would not be able to find her, she thought, relieved. She just had to keep moving. It didn't matter what bit her, what pierced her skin. Whether it was tonight or in the morning, she would respond only when she heard Kumaresan's voice calling out to her: 'Pilla!'

She tried to roll her body tightly into a ball. If she met with an obstacle, she pulled back and looked for somewhere to turn around. She felt that she was getting stronger and stronger. Her heart's desire was to share a long life with Kumaresan. Was she greedy? When she'd realized she was pregnant, she had thought that everything would slowly settle down. Who wouldn't be moved by the sight of a child? She had planned to bear everything patiently until then.

Even when her mother-in-law's words fell on her like lashes from a whip, she had comforted herself thinking all that would change soon. She had never thought that there could be so much evil behind those words. At first glance, this village looked like it was made of a few houses surrounded by a large expanse of land, and that anything could easily enter and get around. But that was an illusion. In truth, not even the wind from elsewhere could enter this space. The air in these parts had circulated within the confines of this place and had turned poisonous. The space would not allow anything to enter. Even Kumaresan did not know this secret.

Had they known things would be like this here, they could have somehow survived in Tholur. Her father and brother were definitely not like these people. They would have been angry with her and Kumaresan, certainly; they might even have hit her, but they would never wish to end their lives.

In Tholur, buildings were close to each other, but the streets were open and wide. They could have lived there happily. A single-room house would have sufficed. Life would have been easier in Virichipalayam too. Perhaps Kumaresan had told someone about his plans to move there, and they had now come to kill her before that could happen. Virichipalayam was a good town. It was the kind of town that welcomed everyone. None of this would have happened had they gone there straight after their wedding. Why hadn't Kumaresan thought of that?

Her movements gained speed. All sorts of thoughts flashed through her mind. If she managed to escape alive, no one would be able to do anything to her. Kumaresan would take her elsewhere to live. He would not want to live with these people any longer. He was not like them; he had never uttered a harsh word to her. He had only ever tried to be a constant source of comfort and confidence. No matter how difficult it was, she had to keep herself alive. In that instant, her heart was suffused with the desire to live.

'Don't go into the bush and get caught in there,' a voice warned the others. 'After all, where can she hide? She will have to come out eventually.'

'I hope Nōndi does not return just yet.'

'Let him come. What can he do? After doing something against the village, does he think he can talk his way out of it?'

'If he comes back and starts objecting, perhaps we should take care of him too. Let's go now. We can see about this in the morning.'

'Yes, let's take care of this in the morning. Where can she go? Who is going to come and get her out!'

'But it is almost morning now.'

'Why postpone this? Let's get this over with.'

'Uncle! The entire bush has dried up. It is only the thorns that look lush on the outside. Why don't we set fire to the bush? We will smoke her out of there.'

'And if she doesn't get smoked out, she can burn and die inside. Yes, let's set fire to it! That's the best idea.'

'That's right. If we set fire from all sides, she will get steamed like a potato inside. Do it.'

Saroja's hands scuttled like rats into whatever crevices she could find. She shrank herself and entered whatever spaces she could access. She didn't feel the pain from the wounds on her body. She did not even think about her clothes being ripped to shreds. Or feel her hair getting caught in the thorns and tearing away. Dried leaves and twigs on the ground rustled and crackled, revealing her presence. Her legs had grown numb after being dragged over sand and stones. She was soaked in perspiration. Seized with the burning desire to save herself by burrowing herself into the sand, she now moved with great urgency.

The noises from the outside started again after a brief respite. She sensed a lot of action at the edges of the bush. Where had all these people come from? Were they the visitors who had come for the chariot festival? Or was her mind playing tricks on her, imagining a person for each sound she heard?

No one was coming towards her. Nothing was happening. She was just lying inside the hut on the rock . . . No, no, she was dreaming, sleeping in her house in Tholur. Everything would vanish if she woke up. Should she wake up and see what happened? But she couldn't wake up. It looked as though she would have to live through this unending torment.

She could see the light from the fire around the bush. It would not take the fire too long to reach her. She could see the flames leaping through the leaves and twigs on the ground like twisting, coiling snakes and ravenously climbing the trees. She was surrounded by light. She felt its hot breath closing in around her.

Her dream would end now. Any moment now she would wake up and laugh at what a terrible dream it was. If she told someone about it, they might even laugh at her. It would be one of those long dreams of which she'd remember every detail.

Enough of this dream.

She tried to wake up. But her eyes kept closing.

All right, there was no other way but to continue with the dream, she decided. This fire was coming to embrace her and release her from some terrible, freezing cold. She readied herself to welcome it with outstretched arms.

At that moment, through the din of sticks cracking and twigs snapping in the fire, she heard the distinct sound of Kumaresan's bicycle approaching.

GLOSSARY

Athai   A kinship term that refers to one's paternal aunt, or mother-in-law, or any female relative or acquaintance who is placed in that status.

Daavani   A long piece of fabric often worn by south Indian girls or women over their torsos, wrapped over a shoulder, with the loose end either hanging free at the back or tied around the waist. It is worn in combination with the pavadai or the long skirt.

Dey!   An affectionate as well as irreverent mode of address where the addressee is a man.

Jaggery   Unrefined sugar made from the sap of palm trees or from sugar cane juice.

Kozhambu   A spicy gravy made with fresh or dried vegetables or fish and tamarind juice, eaten with rice.

Kurma   A side dish made with cooking vegetables or meat in a thick coconut gravy. It is often had along with flavoured rice or bread.

Mapillai   A kinship term often used to refer to a son-in-law or someone who could, within the systems of relationship, possibly be considered a son-in-law. But it is often also used as a term of endearment between men who are peers.

Melam and Nadaswaram   Musical instruments often associated with auspicious occasions. Melam is a two-sided drum played with a stick on one side and with leather knuckle-caps on the other. Nadaswaram is a double-reed wind instrument that is accompanied by the melam.

Poovan   A type of banana grown in the wetlands of south India.

Samba   A small-grained variety of rice grown during the second, long Samba crop season, between August and November, in Tamil Nadu.

TRANSLATOR'S NOTE

I am delighted to have been able to translate yet another of Perumal Murugan's novels. Translating *Maadhorubaagan*, which came out in English as *One Part Woman*, was a tremendous experience. It was a diffuse moment that extended over months as I took up the work in breaks between other tasks—breaks that were meditative, joyous, and humbling. The response to that translation, too, has been intense, not least because of the tide of intolerance and nasty political manoeuvring in the throes of which both the novel and its author were caught.

Translating *Pookkuzhi*—*Pyre*, in English—has been a somewhat different experience. In some ways, it has been more challenging despite the fact that this novel's storyline is more contemporary than that of *Maadhorubaagan*, and it does not dwell so much on mythical and temple narratives. I think the difficulty is because there is more direct speech involved in *Pookkuzhi*; the characters speak a lot and their streams of thought too bear the distinct mark of regional speech patterns. In the Tamil text, Kumaresan's and Saroja's people speak differently; their speech is marked by rural and semi-urban variations. It has been difficult to sustain that difference in translation. Perhaps this is an instance where specificity of language use resists translatability.

In the Tamil text, Perumal Murugan employs a narrative style in which repetitions of phrases or words for the sake of emphasis, and small abrupt shifts back and forth in time without explicit discourse markers are very common. These are aspects of narration that native speakers are, perhaps, accustomed to. But in my translation to English, these sounded unclear and a little confusing, especially given the various ways in which time works in the novel: the psychological time of the characters, especially Saroja's; the past that emerges through memory and reminiscences; her recollections of events that have occurred just a few days ago after her arrival at Kumaresan's village; the time in which stories of Kumaresan's family's past are set, etc. Moreover, since I have developed this habit of producing a very idiomatic translation, there was a good deal of work involved in making the language of translation supple. It could not have happened without the excellent and kind work done by Ambar Sahil Chatterjee, my editor at Penguin India, and Shatarupa Ghoshal, whose copyediting work was meticulous.

There is a taut simplicity to the premise and the plot of this novel. It speaks of love in the face of difference and societal violence. This is a novel about caste and the resilient force that it is, but it is also about how strangely vulnerable caste and its guardians seem to feel in the face of love, and how it often seems to assert itself both in everyday acts of discrimination as well as in moments of most unimaginable violence.

Perumal Murugan seems to have a way of slipping into the emotional space of his characters, especially the women, in an incredibly tender way. Both Saroja and Marayi come through as complex characters with pasts, desires, fears and frustrations. Saroja's misgivings about the prudence of her decision to elope with Kumaresan are as palpable as her constant effort not to give voice to them.

His important male protagonists too, like Kali in *Maadhorubaagan* and Kumaresan here, are loving and kind, certainly men of their times but also men who rage *against* their times. All his characters seem extremely believable to me, very singular yet reminding us of people we might know, shining with the possibility that we could find them, or people like them, out in the 'real' world.

Although I am a native Tamil speaker, the particularities of the Kongu dialects did lead to some moments of doubts and anxiety. Theodore Baskaran came to my aid when I needed it most.

Kannan Sundaram of Kalachuvadu Publications, who has published both *Maadhorubaagan* and *Pookkuzhi*, has shown a very steady confidence in me, which has helped in times of acute self-doubt.

It is an act of trust on Perumal Murugan's part to let me translate his work. There is something life-affirming about the kindness and love with which he approaches his characters, the warmth with which he treats them. His works invite vulnerability on the part of the readers and draw us into their rich details of life, landscape, ecology and social life of a region. It is an honour to have opportunities to interact with him and serve as a kind of medium, albeit an imperfect one, through which some of his novels reach a different readership.

—Aniruddhan Vasudevan
February 14, 2016
Austin, Texas

Perumal Murugan is one of India's most respected and highest selling literary writers, author of eleven novels and five collections each of short stories and poetry. He was born in rural Tamil Nadu, where he continues to live and work. He has twice been longlisted for the National Book Award for Translated Literature for *One Part Woman* and *The Story of a Goat*, both of which are published by Pushkin Press.

Aniruddhan Vasudevan writes and translates between Tamil and English. His translations include *One Part Woman*, *A Lonely Harvest*, and *Trial by Silence* by Perumal Murugan, and *A Night with a Black Spider* by Ambai.

ONE PART WOMAN

Perumal Murugan

Translated by Aniruddhan Vasudevan

'*One Part Woman* contains the sweetest, most substantial portrait of an Indian marriage in recent fiction'
Karan Mahajan

'Intimate and affecting . . . Throughout the novel, Murugan pits the individual against the group. How far are you willing to go, he asks, in order to belong?'
New York Times Book Review

Kali and Ponna are perfectly content in their marriage, aside from one thing: they are unable to conceive. As their childlessness begins to attract local gossip and family disapproval, they consider a drastic plan: The annual chariot festival is approaching. For one night during the festival celebrating the half male, half-female god Maadhorubaagan, the rules of marriage are relaxed, and consensual sex between unmarried men and women is overlooked, for all men are considered gods. But rather than bringing them together, this scheme threatens to drive the couple apart.

Selling over 100,000 copies in India, where it was published first in the original Tamil and then in this celebrated English translation, *One Part Woman* has become a cult phenomenon in the subcontinent, jump-starting conversations about caste and female empowerment.

THE STORY OF A GOAT

Perumal Murugan

Translated by N. Kalyan Raman

'An affecting story told with sensitivity towards the plight of the individual and calm fury at society's brutality'

Irish Times

'Jumps nimbly from fantasy to realism to parable . . . The elegance of Murugan's simple tone will lull you deeper into his story'

Washington Post

Poonachi is the runt of the litter, a small black kid goat left in mysterious circumstances with an elderly farmer and his wife. Although the little goats seems too frail to survive, they take her in and raise her. Soon she is bounding with joy and growing at a miraculous rate.

But there is danger behind every corner; as the seasons turn, poverty, drought and an authoritarian government cast a long shadow over Poonachi's isolated village. Is this little goat too humble a creature to survive in such a hostile world?